ME
EQ FACTOR

MEASURE YOUR EQ FACTOR

*Discover and Develop
Your Emotional Potential*

Gilles d'Ambra

foulsham
LONDON • NEW YORK • TORONTO • SYDNEY

foulsham

The Publishing House, Bennetts Close,
Slough, Berkshire, SL1 5AP, England.

ISBN 0-572-02538-6

This English language edition © 2000 W. Foulsham & Co. Ltd
Originally published by Marabout (Belgique) © 1997.

Front cover phtoograph © The Stock Market Photo Agency Inc.

Printed in Great Britain by Cox & Wyman Ltd, Reading.

CONTENTS

INTRODUCTION

The major revolution of the twenty-first century is going to be a drastic shift in favour of the importance of the emotions and away from reliance on pure reason. Understanding and developing your emotional intelligence will be the key to success in both your professional and personal life.

What is EQ?
Our EQ, or emotional intelligence quotient, is, by definition, complex because it combines many different qualities, often almost indiscernible from each other, such as self-awareness, the ability to read our own feelings, control our impulses and communicate with others. It cannot be quantified in the same way as IQ. It needs to be evaluated in terms of our self-awareness and our relationships with others.

This book offers you the means to evaluate your own emotional quotient.

It contains 21 tests that will allow you to explore your personality, both private and public, to discover your emotional psychostyle and to assess your relationships with others, particularly in the areas of relationships between men and women and of your love life.

Each of the tests will give you a precise insight into different facets of your emotional intelligence, as well as advice on how to make improvements that will benefit your relationships.

All the tests were originally published in *Elle* magazine.

PART I

EXPLORE YOUR PERSONALITY

Everyone has an instinctive idea of their emotional intelligence but the following eight tests will help you to define more accurately the different aspects of your personality.

In the personal sphere, you will discover your degrees of sensuality and your passionate inclinations; you will also be able to evaluate your level of sentimentality and your attitudes to fidelity.

In the social sphere, they will measure your independence and sociability, your levels of ambition and assertiveness.

Study each statement and choose the response that most closely matches your own feelings. Write down all your scores; later, they will be used to help you to discover your emotional psychostyle.

ARE YOU SENSUAL?

> **SCORE:**
> 2 points for each A answer
> 1 point for each B answer
> 0 points for each C answer
>
> Add up the totals and look up the profile that corresponds to your score on pages 13–15.

You would like to make love in a bath full of:
- A Olive oil (freshly pressed, of course).
- B Fresh creamy milk.
- C Dom Pérignon champagne.

Before making love, you always like to:
- A Smoke a joint.
- B Have a drink.
- C Brush your teeth.

Love-making is much better:
- A Without a condom.
- B With a condom.
- C Either way – you don't feel any difference.

Look at your lips. Would you say that:
- A They are equally plump.
- B The lower lip is fuller than the upper lip.
- C They are both rather thin.

The most erotic place to make love would be:
- A In the kitchen.
- B On a train.
- C In the open air.

When there is a full moon:
- A   You feel very unsettled.
- B   You are not quite yourself.
- C   You don't feel any different.

You have a soft spot for:
- A   Chocolate.
- B   Yoghurt.
- C   Salad.

It makes you shiver just to think about:
- A   Wasps.
- B   Snakes.
- C   Spiders, especially the big hairy ones.

You would find it absolutely disgusting to:
- A   Drink a glass of olive oil.
- B   Swallow a raw egg.
- C   Chew boiled milk skin.

When it comes to wearing perfume:
- A   You use only two or three perfumes.
- B   You always use the same one.
- C   You often change your perfume.

At breakfast, you eat your toast:
- A   With lots of butter and marmalade.
- B   With a scraping of low-fat spread.
- C   You rarely eat toast for breakfast.

You would most enjoy going to:
- A   A horse race.
- B   A rock concert.
- C   A porno show.

You are most distressed by:
- A   Being trapped in the middle of a crowd.
- B   Looking over the edge of a sheer cliff.
- C   The sight of blood.

Your favourite time of day is:
>   A   Early morning, when everything is fresh.
>   B   The middle of the night, when everybody is asleep.
>   C   Dusk.

A platonic friendship with someone of the opposite sex is:
>   A   Absolutely unthinkable.
>   B   Always a bit dodgy.
>   C   Quite natural.

If you could take on a supernatural appearance, you would like to be a:
>   A   Werewolf.
>   B   Vampire.
>   C   Ghost.

You most often dream of:
>   A   Flying.
>   B   Falling.
>   C   Being naked.

Thinking back to your childhood, you find it easiest to remember:
>   A   Places.
>   B   Smells.
>   C   People (apart from your parents).

Your star sign is:
>   A   Cancer, Scorpio, Pisces, Taurus.
>   B   Aries, Leo, Sagittarius, Virgo.
>   C   Gemini, Libra, Aquarius, Capricorn.

You tend to cry a lot when you are:
>   A   Listening to music.
>   B   At the cinema.
>   C   Reading a love story.

If you have scored 0 to 13 points
Your head rules your heart – you could say that everything seems to be governed by your neurones and hardly anything by your hormones. You are not particularly in touch with your body and you pay scant attention to your feelings.

You don't let yourself live much. Your lifestyle tends to be rather Spartan, with the emphasis on self-denial; you tend to go for strict diets and you could even be anorexic. You prefer to see things rather than feel them and you may react badly to unusual stimuli, such as a flavour that is unfamiliar or a smell that's too strong. You are very sure of the things you like – although they have a tendency to be rather bland – and you can be almost phobic about the things you don't like.

Your world tends to be rather sterile and more or less closed to anything new. You wouldn't think of walking barefoot in the early morning dew, or wallowing in a mud bath, unless it's for purely practical reasons. You're not really into cream cakes or French kisses. And as far as sex goes, it's not something you luxuriate in – it's all too messy. Indulging in anything wild or really letting your hair down in a moment of sheer madness is not for you.

Long periods of abstinence don't bother you – sex just isn't essential for you and you can go without it. Your appetites and desires tend to be more spiritual, cultural (you are probably a bookworm), or strictly practical (you get great satisfaction from a job well done). You probably feel quite content with life but it would do no harm to indulge yourself occasionally. Buy yourself a box of chocolates (and eat them all) or have a massage. Everyone deserves the odd treat.

If you have scored 14 to 27 points
You feel good about yourself – your spirit and body live happily together. Your senses are a source of many pleasures to you. You know how to sink voluptuously into the depths of a sofa and allow yourself to be carried away by music or by someone of the opposite sex. You enjoy comfort and take advantage of the good times.

Sensually, you are very open and you appreciate contrasts and diversity. You don't mind trying new, strong flavours and you have the same appetite for good food as for good sex. Generally speaking, you are well in control of yourself and even when you do overindulge, you know when to stop. Curiosity is a feature of your personality as you want to try out all kinds of sensations, although you don't let your desire for pleasure take over.

You are sensitive to people and situations and if you are ever conned, it's because you ignore the alarm signals – you should always trust your first impressions. Sexually, like everyone else, you have your ups and downs, but being celibate for too long depresses you. There is a limit to your body's patience! For you, life without sex is unimaginable, and love without desire is quite out of the question.

If you have scored 28 to 40 points

You are sensual to your very fingertips. Your body leads the orchestra of your senses (admittedly with the occasional false note). You are deeply voluptuous, you tend to look for and try anything that will satisfy your sensuality. Your desires come first, and you don't look any further than your body's pleasures. 'I want to' is your favourite refrain. You are forever being tempted by one thing or another, from ice cream to the barman.

Naturally, you hate being frustrated. Your desires have to be satisfied immediately and you loathe having to wait for anything; you can be imperious, you don't like anyone saying no to you; and, as you cannot satisfy all your own desires (who can?), you are often disappointed. You may react by overindulging yourself (especially if your score is closer to 40) with food, alcohol and tobacco (you have a great need for oral satisfaction), beauty treatments or clothes (you are often a fashion victim). Sex certainly plays a central role in your life. You can't go without it. Not for long, anyway. A month of celibacy for you seems an eternity. Ever hungry for love, you often mistake strong physical sensations for true emotional feelings. You tend to confuse desire with love, which has a detrimental effect on all your relationships. Perhaps you should try to be less self-indulgent. After all, none of us can have everything we want, when we want it, and if you demand too much, you will end up being permanently disappointed. The less you expect, the more satisfied you will be with what you have; and once you value what you have, you will be less inclined to chase after things you don't really need.

ARE YOU PASSIONATE?

> **SCORE:**
> 2 points for each A answer
> 1 point for each B answer
> 0 points for each C answer
>
> Add up the totals and look up the profile that corresponds to your score on pages 19–21.

The greatest pleasures are:
- A The ones you most expect.
- B The most unusual.
- C The ones that take you completely by surprise.

Right now:
- A You are in love.
- B You would like to be in love.
- C You have other priorities.

True love:
- A Can only happen once in a lifetime.
- B Is a miracle every time it happens.
- C Is just a big illusion.

The worst thing about love is:
- A One person in the relationship always loves more than the other.
- B When it stops, you both end up asking yourselves if you ever were really in love.
- C Sooner or later, it always ends.

The last time you made love without really feeling like it, it was:
- A Because you didn't want to be alone.
- B Something you never want to repeat.
- C Because you wanted to please someone.

You felt you had grown up:
- A When you met your first love.
- B When you left home.
- C The first time you were let down in love.

Your loved one says: 'I don't feel like sex at the moment'. You think this means:
- A 'I don't love you any more.'
- B He has some kind of problem.
- C Nothing – he never does feel like it very much.

You would find it difficult to forgive, if he forgot:
- A The first time you met.
- B Valentine's Day.
- C Your birthday.

If you were jealous, you would:
- A Follow him to see where he goes.
- B Go through his pockets.
- C Check the messages on his answering machine.

Your worst nightmare is when you dream about:
- A Losing your teeth.
- B Being chased by something.
- C The walls closing in on you.

The doorbell rings and you are not expecting anyone. You think it's:
- A Your ex pestering you.
- B A registered letter.
- C An encyclopaedia salesman.

As a child, you tended to:
- A Collect things.
- B Throw occasional tantrums.
- C Play by yourself a lot.

Your present job is:
- A Wonderful – you love everything about it.
- B Not exactly your dream job, but it will do.
- C Just a way of earning a living.

Life is like sport; the important thing is:
- A Winning.
- B Taking part.
- C Not coming last.

In a team situation, you tend to be the one who will:
- A Come up with an idea or a plan.
- B Reconcile the different points of view.
- C Find a real solution to a problem.

You are particularly sensitive to changes:
- A In your own mood.
- B In the mood of those close to you.
- C In the weather.

The most important thing to teach children is that they must:
- A Do what they want when they want.
- B Cope by themselves.
- C Pay for their mistakes.

To increase your pleasure, you would be most likely to say:
- A 'Hurt me a little ...'
- B 'Hold me tight ...'
- C 'More ...'

If you felt you had been betrayed in love, you would kill:
- A Your partner.
- B Your rival.
- C Yourself.

As a couple, you argue:
- A Almost every day.
- B At least once a week.
- C Rarely more than once a month.

If you have scored 0 to 13 points
You do not have mad crushes or crazes on things or people. You are rather cool, and tend to view life with a calm detachment; your emotions are rarely ruffled. 'Live and let live' is your philosophy. You are not the type to fight for your ideals and when you do get involved, your approach is always practical.

You claim not to get emotional about things – and you never (or almost never) seem to. You heart doesn't melt when someone pays you a compliment; you don't get upset if someone criticises you. You are not the type of woman to get passionate about anything: you don't find that overnight you've developed an irresistible urge to spend hours talking to people on the Internet; you wouldn't suddenly throw out all your sensible knickers and replace them with leopardskin-patterned thongs. Your likes and dislikes are fairly set and you don't suddenly change your mind about the way you feel. You are constant in your affections, your ideas and your ambitions.

When it comes to marriage, your head rules your heart. You are wary of sudden thrills, and are unlikely to be blinded by passion. You know that love can have a destructive side to it and so you tend to treat a new affair with caution, preferring to remain clear-headed and practical. You feel a need to let your relationships develop gradually, basing them on long-lasting and long-held feelings. It is highly unlikely that you would ever let yourself be carried away by strong sexual attraction.

If you have scored 14 to 27 points
There's more desire for action than passion in you. You do fall in love, and you are capable of getting carried away with a new idea or project. You may suddenly decide that you simply have to learn to play the piano or golf, or speak Chinese. Or you may give up everything overnight, to follow the one you love to the ends of the earth.

You are never indifferent or lukewarm about anything; you would never say 'So what? – I've seen it all before'. And yet you would never launch into something without checking it out first. You can be spontaneous but you don't fall for things hook, line and sinker and you always like to know there's a way out. You may adore tennis, country rock or Italian shoes, but you know you can do without them. You would never put all your eggs in one basket – so you certainly wouldn't get yourself in a state because a man dumped you. You usually bounce right back after any kind of setback, disappointment or unsuccessful love affair. Spending time feeling sorry for yourself is not your style (not for too long, anyway) and you don't hang on to the past – you want to get on with life.

If you have scored 28 to 40 points

You are often the victim of sudden infatuations and irresistible desire. You live in an atmosphere of tension, excitement and urgency. Any minute you may develop a craze for cycling or salsa music or pre-Socratic philosophy. One look from a pair of blue eyes can have you falling hopelessly in love, and you'll hand over your house keys to someone you've barely met. You tend to get hooked on things too easily – sport, sex, work – and, because you are intellectually and emotionally dependent, you are easily influenced by fashion or other people.

The frustration of waiting when you want something is unbearable, but once you get it, you often lose interest. You tend to get bored quickly with routine. New interests, fresh stimulation and excitement are what you need. You also tend to dramatise every situation, every relationship, everything that happens to you.

You are very jealous of your partners and your friends and this jealousy may be uncontrollable (especially if your score is closer to 40 points). You go from one extreme to the other, from ecstasy to anxiety, from elation to depression, from adulation to loathing. Your relationships are always on the verge of breaking up and you live in a constant round of arguing and making up again.

You need to get into the habit of looking before you leap – you are inclined to be too quick to rush into things without thinking. Learn to take a deep breath instead of reacting with a hurtful retort that you may regret. Stand still and listen to what your partner has to say instead of simply exploding with rage. Stop and think first, whether you are considering spending hundreds of pounds on equipment because you fancy scuba-diving, or cutting up your partner's suits because you saw him having lunch with another woman. The little time it takes may save you a lot of heartache in the long run. After all, you may find you hate getting water in your ears, and it might have been his sister.

ARE YOU SENTIMENTAL?

SCORE:
2 points for each A answer
1 point for each B answer
0 points for each C answer

Add up the totals and look up the profile that corresponds to your score on pages 25–7.

You always carry with you at least one photo of:
  A Your family.
  B Your loved one.
  C You don't bother carrying photos.

You made love for the first time when you were:
  A Under 15.
  B Between 15 and 18.
  C Over 18.

Valentine's Day is on:
  A February 14.
  B February 12.
  C March 7.

You often think about:
  A Your childhood.
  B Your ex.
  C Your last holiday.

The most effective way to hold on to the one you love is to:
  A Pray.
  B Make him a nice meal.
  C Cast a spell on him.

You hate being apart because:
- A He doesn't call every day.
- B You don't know when you are going to see him again.
- C He doesn't leave a number.

You find it more difficult to:
- A Hide your feelings.
- B Be sure of your feelings.
- C Pretend to be feeling something that isn't there.

The last time you cried was:
- A Three days ago.
- B More than a week ago.
- C More than a month ago.

The most beautiful love letter you have ever read is:
- A The very first one you received.
- B The last one you wrote.
- C The last one you received.

If you haven't heard from your latest man for three days, you:
- A Brood in a corner.
- B Throw yourself into your work.
- C Try to forget your sorrows by having a good time.

If he leaves you, saying, 'Let's leave things open', it means:
- A 'He doesn't dare tell me that he doesn't love me any more.'
- B 'He doesn't know if he wants to see me again.'
- C 'He'll see me if he has nothing better to do.'

When you have had a few drinks, you tend to:
- A Feel depressed.
- B Become euphoric.
- C Become aggressive.

When you have problems with your love life, you:
- A Eat chocolate.
- B Don't sleep at all well.
- C Lose your appetite.

You have more of a talent for:
    A Speaking foreign languages.
    B Playing sport.
    C Solving practical problems.

You often:
    A Feel uneasy at parties.
    B Do things by habit.
    C Do one thousand things at once.

At work, you would like:
    A More recognition for your efforts.
    B More interesting tasks.
    C More money.

When watching a tennis match, you always support:
    A The player who is losing.
    B The one you fancy more.
    C The favourite.

If a clairvoyant predicts a 'happy event', it must mean:
    A A baby.
    B An encounter.
    C A wedding.

In your home, you like to have:
    A Lots of flowers and plants.
    B At least one houseplant.
    C A few nice vases.

To save your neck in court, you would plead:
    A A crime of passion.
    B Diminished responsibility.
    C 'It was an accident, your Honour'.

If you have scored 0 to 13 points

You are more pragmatic than really sentimental. With you, emotions come second. You are not the type to keep old love letters and photos in a suitcase, imagining that one day you will show them to your grandchildren. Other people's misfortunes don't easily move you (you don't even feel sorry for yourself that often) and you certainly don't cry for nothing.

That doesn't stop you from having feelings, but you reserve them for very specific people or circumstances. On the whole, you try to be objective and logical. Even when it comes to your relationships with family and friends, you think very carefully about your actions instead of letting your heart tell you what to do. You are not much of a psychologist in your dealings with others; you tend to be rather short on understanding – you are just too practical. You simply can't see, for example, why anyone would want to hang on to their old childhood teddy bear. You lack empathy. You tend to rationalise too much, to be too critical. You would get more out of your relationships if you could allow your emotions to show a little more, and to be guided by them.

In love, you are reluctant to get involved unless you are sure of being loved. You are not often very demonstrative and you find it difficult to express your feelings or be openly loving or affectionate. Even when you are deeply involved in a love relationship, there's always a degree of self-consciousness stopping you from being spontaneous, from completely letting yourself go. You need to learn to take risks with your emotions – there is so much happiness to be won and, who knows, you may find you can enjoy the thrill of danger too.

If you have scored 14 to 27 points

You are a sentimental soul. Emotions and feelings are very important to you. You approach things subjectively and you are very intuitive of people and situations. You place more emphasis on style than logic.

In your everyday life, your views are based more on your personal values and motivations than on practicalities. In your personal life, the most important thing for you is a harmonious relationship with someone. You enjoy company and in a group situation you are a thoughtful listener and adviser, someone who can arbitrate and reconcile people's different attitudes and interests.

You are able (especially if your score is closer to 40) to put yourself in other people's shoes and you find it easy to tune in to other people's feelings as you are very good at sensing other people's moods and reactions and you are rarely insensitive to the problems of others. On the other hand, you are often uncomfortable when faced with personal conflict. You tend to avoid it, even though it may mean agreeing with a friend when you think they are in the wrong or giving in to your partner's wishes rather than saying what **you** really want.

Tender expressions of love are very important to you and you readily demonstrate them yourself. In your relationships, you and your partner attend to each other's every need. You care about each other's mental and physical comfort. You are not at all the sort who relishes heart-rending, rollercoaster affairs. You need to feel a sense of well-being and have peace of mind.

If you have scored 28 to 40 points
You are excessively sentimental (especially if your score is closer to 40). You tend to let yourself be taken over by emotions, to be held hostage to other people's feelings. You easily and quickly become very fond of people. Your heart is always ready to feel something for everyone – but, unfortunately, in reality it means nothing. You frequently display emotions you don't really feel. You can embrace someone you have just met as if they were the love of your life and you can sob uncontrollably at the sight of Bambi lost in the forest. Whatever the situation, you always tend to overreact.

Unfortunately, this means that you cannot distinguish between nit-picking criticism and constructive personal appraisal. If someone tells you that you have made a mistake, you think 'I am useless.' You are hypersensitive to events around you; your moods and your feelings are easily affected. This excessive sensitivity may hold you back in your work and in your relationships. You may appear self-confident but deep down have no confidence in yourself at all. In company you are probably not happy unless you are sure that you are the centre of attention.

You are also rather self-centred in your love affairs and, although you think you give a lot, you are prey to jealousy and envy. You quickly become dependent on people and are frequently tormented by the fear of being abandoned.

You need to try not to be so hard on yourself. Stop taking other people's opinions so much to heart and try to value yourself more – it will help your self-confidence.

ARE YOU FAITHFUL?

SCORE:
2 points for each A answer
1 point for each B answer
0 points for each C answer

Add up the totals and look up the profile that corresponds to
your score on pages 31–3.

You still keep in touch with:

    A Your secondary school friends.
    B Old work colleagues.
    C Your ex.

You call your mother:

    A Almost every day.
    B At least once a week.
    C Rarely more than once a month.

You pray:

    A Often.
    B Sometimes.
    C Never.

The longest you have ever gone without sex was:

    A More than six months.
    B Three months.
    C One month.

In your relationships, jealousy is:

    A A game.
    B A spice.
    C A poison.

You are out walking with your partner when you come face to face with someone he seems to know very well. He doesn't introduce you, so:
- A You wait patiently to one side.
- B Feeling uncomfortable, you discreetly slip away.
- C You introduce yourself anyway.

You always want to slap your partner when he accuses you of:
- A Forgetting things.
- B Being too selfish.
- C Lying.

When you think about your first love:
- A You always remember him with nostalgia.
- B You can't even remember why you broke up.
- C The memory of his face is a blur.

You know the two of you are going through a crisis when:
- A You can't talk honestly to each other.
- B Your life seems dreary.
- C You make love less and less frequently.

He lands in your heart and in your life with a child you don't like very much. You think:
- A It won't stop you from becoming a real family.
- B You will learn to love the child.
- C You will show patience.

Your ideal man is someone who, when the chips are down, will above all be faithful to:
- A His principles.
- B His feelings.
- C His commitments.

To your mind, you are unfaithful if:
- A You dream about someone else.
- B You are tempted by someone else.
- C You think about someone else whilst making love.

Most of your decisions are based on:
- A Firm beliefs.
- B Intuitions.
- C Doubts.

When you vote, you vote for:
- A An ideal.
- B A person.
- C You don't vote.

You are particularly grateful to your parents for having taught you to:
- A Respect certain values.
- B Work hard.
- C Behave well.

If you were an artist, you would be a:
- A Musician.
- B Writer.
- C Comedian.

As a child:
- A You always went to sleep without any problem.
- B You had to have the light on to go to sleep.
- C You used to look under the bed before getting in it.

You chose your job:
- A Because it's your vocation.
- B To please your parents.
- C Because of a combination of circumstances.

If you were offered a council flat you are not entitled to, you would:
- A Refuse, thinking about all those who really need it.
- B Accept, because it would otherwise only go to someone who doesn't deserve it any more than you do.
- C Accept unreservedly; you would never say no to a good deal.

Over the last 20 years you have changed:
   A Not much.
   B For the better.
   C Into someone quite different.

If you have scored 0 to 13 points
You have little constancy in your affections, your feelings or your opinions. You are unlikely to be faithful (even less so if your score is closer to 0) to your promises, your habits or your beliefs. You are rather the sort of person who has fads and fancies, and changes her mind, opinion or direction at the drop of a hat.

You are often able to forget about your morals when it suits your own personal interests, give up your principles just for the sake of peace and quiet – you're an opportunist. If necessary, you can take advantage of a situation without feeling too many twinges of conscience (and sometimes none at all). Faced with having to make a choice, the little voice inside you always tells you that if you don't like the decision you make, you can wriggle your way out, turn things around so that you can have your cake and eat it. Truth is always relative with you, and lying and insincerity are almost second nature – you believe that the end (suiting yourself) always justifies the means and you never give a straight answer if you can avoid it.

In your love affairs, you are a polygamist at heart and it's not because your hormones are working overtime. It's just that you can't seem to be happy with one person or commit yourself to just one relationship. You can't help yourself from wanting to have – or actually having – several relationships at the same time and you frequently change partners. Your promises to be faithful are only valid whilst you are making them. There and then you may mean it, but as soon as you are out of the door ...

Your selfishness and lack of moral code are all very well in the short term and you are probably having quite a lot of fun for now, but you may find that your behaviour will earn you few lasting friendships.

Perhaps it's time to start thinking about changing your outlook a little before you start losing friends.

If you have scored 14 to 27 points
You are pretty much true to yourself. Of course you have your flings and fancies and you change your mind a bit. You don't stick to favourite brands and you don't always keep your word. You give in to the occasional weakness and you will tell a little white lie when it suits you. But generally you regard loyalty, honesty and sincerity as ideal values that have been fixed in you since childhood, and you really do try hard to stick to them.

You'd rather not break your promises or betray your convictions or affections, and although you are prepared to be flexible where necessary, you would never compromise your conscience. You have confidence in what you believe, and fidelity and romanticism are the basis of your belief in love.

Married or otherwise, you need to love and be loved in an exclusive relationship and this is as much to suit yourself as to conform socially. It may happen that you are unfaithful or you may have to accept that someone has been unfaithful to you but you are not one of those people who imagines that it can strengthen a relationship, and you refuse to make it a way of life. You don't see yourself either deliberately committing adultery or turning a blind eye to it.

If you have scored 27 to 40 points
You're not just faithful, you have a rigid, unbending attitude that is almost fanatical. You have an overactive conscience and too many moral scruples. For you, any promise or commitment is sacred. You feel guilty even at the thought of not being able to honour one yourself and the slightest failure to do so on someone else's part would make you so bitter and angry, you could not forgive them.

You may be so rooted to your convictions and your habits, you are incapable of relaxing your views. You tend to attach too much importance to principles and hardly any to feelings, whether they be your own or other people's. You persist in pursuing your ideas and are quite unable to moderate your attitude, let alone change your mind about something. Sometimes you may be obstinate beyond reason and you often have a real problem with compromise and forgiveness.

The positive side of all this is that you are very much on the level. You have no hidden agenda, no dirty tricks up your sleeve – people know exactly where they stand with you. You may often take a long time to make up your mind or commit yourself but, once you have, things are definite, pretty well set in stone.

In your love affairs, you are straightforward, tough and often fiercely jealous. Ideally, you are a one-man woman. You dream about absolute, exclusive, definitive love. But be warned, in real life, as you will discover, people change and what you thought was true love may often let you down.

If you are to avoid constant disappointment and heartbreak, you will have to understand that this is not necessarily evidence of disloyalty. After all, not everyone has your rigid moral fibre. But you must realise that change is an essential part of nature; as life around you evolves and circumstances alter, try to learn to bend and change and develop yourself too. You don't have to give up your principles: just learn to make allowances for human nature.

ARE YOU INDEPENDENT?

SCORE:
2 points for each A answer
1 point for each B answer
0 points for each C answer

Add up the totals and look up the profile that corresponds to your score on pages 37–9.

Your partner dumps you for someone else. You:
  A Are prepared to humiliate yourself to get him back.
  B Respect his decision.
  C Feel strangely relieved.

You are happy to go alone:
  A To the cinema.
  B To eat in a restaurant.
  C On holiday abroad.

When it comes to driving:
  A You don't have a licence.
  B You like the freedom of having your own car.
  C You also have a motorcycle licence.

In your teens, your parents left you fairly free to:
  A Choose your friends.
  B Choose your studies.
  C Go where you wanted in the evening or at weekends.

When you don't see anybody for a day:
  A You feel a little lost.
  B It gives you the chance to recover from your mad social life.
  C You relish the peace and quiet.

At a party, if you set eyes on someone you like, you:
- A Don't leave him alone for a minute.
- B Wait for a sign of interest from him.
- C Hook him straight away.

If you have a problem with someone at work, you:
- A Do nothing and hope that things will get better.
- B Immediately ask for a frank explanation.
- C Decide to have nothing to do with them.

When your Hoover makes worrying noises, you:
- A Assume it's quite normal, it's always done that.
- B Call the repairman.
- C Fetch your tool kit.

When it comes to boring chores, either at work or at home, you:
- A Often volunteer to do them.
- B Do your bit but no more.
- C Always find a way of getting out of doing them.

At work, you are more efficient when:
- A You have a well-defined role within a team.
- B You are given work and then left to get on with it.
- C You work alone.

You have a blazing row and fall out with your best friend. You are sure:
- A It's for the best.
- B Everything will get sorted out in time.
- C You really asked for it.

Your butcher likes to make offensive racist remarks, so:
- A You ignore them, it's not your problem.
- B You boycott him.
- C You become a vegetarian.

When it came to choosing your current home:
- A He chose it for you.
- B You chose it together.
- C You chose it.

When you are out with other people:
- A You often ask yourself what they find interesting about you.
- B You have the feeling you are well liked.
- C You don't care much what they think about you.

You are stuck at home waiting for your latest boyfriend to call, so:
- A You don't dare take a shower or hoover the carpets in case you don't hear the phone.
- B You use the time to do some washing or watch a video.
- C You let your answering machine do its job.

When your last love affair broke up:
- A You thought about killing yourself.
- B You were expecting it really.
- C You were the one who finished it.

You decide to live together; you think it would be perfect:
- A For you to move into his place.
- B To find something together.
- C For him to move into your place.

If a relationship is going to work, it's important to:
- A Do everything together.
- B Have separate interests.
- C Be able to go out to dinner with an ex without it being a drama.

You often find that you:
- A Wait by the phone if you are expecting your man to ring.
- B Ask his advice on your clothes.
- C Let him choose where you go for dinner or which film you go and see.

You dream of becoming (or you already are):
- A A civil servant.
- B A head of department.
- C Your own boss.

If you have scored 0 to 13 points

You are almost entirely dependent on others and seem to be virtually incapable of making a decision by yourself. In your everyday life, you are always asking other people everything from 'What shall I wear?' to 'Should I take that new job?' You find it difficult to choose your holiday destination or the colour for your sofa. You need reassurance and approval in everything you do and the little self-confidence you do have tends to collapse at the slightest reproach or criticism.

You often panic at the idea of being left to your own devices. To avoid being rejected, as you see it, you are prepared to believe anything you're told, so you tend to turn a blind eye to others' faults. You find yourself going along with things even when you don't agree or you don't feel like it. Even worse, you will do all the dirty work and sacrifice your own enjoyment just to be loved. You are always looking for a partner who will give you the protection and support you think you need, even when this may mean allowing yourself be dominated.

You need to realise that your own opinions are just as valid as everyone else's. Try to remember that everyone can make mistakes and that if you do, it doesn't detract from your value as a person. Your real friends will love you for who you are, not what you do for them – and, far from rejecting you, they'll probably be delighted if you try to do things without them occasionally.

If you have scored 14 to 27 points

You are quite self-contained and manage your life quite well. To get on with others, you are prepared to compromise a little, but it would be out of the question for you to give up your whole personality. You have your own definite tastes and opinions and when you don't agree, you say so (not always very politely). After all, in your opinion you shouldn't have to live your life striving for other people's approval (or disapproval).

You are open to suggestions and you listen to the different sides of a story, but in the end, you always make your own decisions and take responsibility for them. You don't need anybody to hold your hand and you certainly don't need someone to tell you what to do or where to go. You have enough confidence in yourself to be able to cope alone – your world doesn't stand still if you're left by yourself. If your flatmate has something to do without you at a weekend, you don't feel lost. You have your own life, your own interests, your own friends.

The same goes for your relationships. As far as you're concerned, being part of a couple doesn't mean being joined at the hip. Of course, you believe you should always be conscious of each other's needs, but that doesn't stop you from doing your own thing or going out at night with your friends if you want to.

If you have scored 28 to 40 points
You're rather overdoing this independence thing. You think you are independent because you do what you want, the way you want, when you want. You say that you don't need anybody to hold your hand, ever. You claim to be comfortable when there's no one special in your life and the idea of spending a weekend alone doesn't bother you. But despite the fact that you talk to your mother on the phone every evening and make a point of keeping in touch with your ex, the reality is that you are tending to make yourself isolated from other people.

You don't really go in for sharing, particularly on an emotional level. All your relationships are rather one-way (you take a lot but give little) and often superficial (you want to have fun but you don't want the problems of getting involved). You tend to put yourself first and you would probably not give up your emotional and physical comforts for the sake of a friend or even for love unless you were forced to. For you, sharing your life with someone would mean pressure and frustration, and in your love affairs, you quickly feel stifled and may become easily annoyed. Faced with the necessity of having to make compromises, you often find it much simpler to withdraw and end the relationship.

For all that, your efforts to maintain your independent stance are really only making you rather isolated and possibly lonely. Suiting yourself is all very well, but you might find that, if you made a little space for others in your life, it would bring all kinds of benefits. After all, it's quite nice to be needed by someone else, once in a while.

ARE YOU SOCIABLE?

> **SCORE:**
> 2 points for each A answer
> 1 point for each B answer
> 0 points for each C answer
>
> Add up the totals and look up the profile that corresponds to your score on pages 43–4.

You are:
- A   An only child.
- B   One of several children in your family.
- C   The youngest.

At lunchtime at work, you usually:
- A   Eat a sandwich on your own.
- B   Go with a friend to the small café on the corner.
- C   Go to the pub with a group of your work colleagues.

When you are out driving and someone cuts you up:
- A   You ignore it.
- B   You mutter a few insults under your breath.
- C   You hurl abuse and give him a V-sign.

In the chicken and egg dilemma, you would give priority to:
- A   The egg.
- B   The chicken.
- C   Neither.

Most of the time, your desk at work is:
- A   Empty.
- B   Tidy, with everything in neat piles.
- C   A paper jungle.

You feel most distressed when you have problems:
 A With your man.
 B With your parents.
 C With people at work.

In a meeting, you tend to:
 A Wait for the right moment to say your piece.
 B Try to agree with everything to calm things down.
 C Make a fool of yourself by talking too much.

If your dentist keeps you waiting:
 A You slip away after 15 minutes to escape the whole thing.
 B You patiently wait your turn.
 C You take the opportunity to get to know everyone in the waiting room.

A traffic policeman stops you because you jumped a red light. You tell him:
 A 'It's your fault, I was distracted by the sight of you.'
 B 'Fair enough.'
 C 'I did it on purpose.'

Your boss reprimands you for acting without consulting him. You reply:
 A 'You weren't here, so I thought I should take the initiative.'
 B 'I thought you said it was all right.'
 C 'We had to do something.'

Your mother-in-law invites you to lunch yet again so you:
 A Say you are too tired.
 B Invent a prior engagement.
 C Put it off until the following Sunday.

The thing you hate most about telephones is:
 A Getting an answering machine.
 B Never-ending conversations.
 C Days without a phone call.

You think top models are:
- A Artificial.
- B Inaccessible.
- C Irritating.

You would not choose to go to:
- A An amusement park.
- B A theatre.
- C A museum.

The best reason for getting married is:
- A To make the relationship official.
- B To have children.
- C To have a party.

It would be worst to be caught crying by:
- A Your children.
- B Your friends.
- C Your colleagues.

You would most enjoy a weekend at:
- A A hotel.
- B Your parents' home.
- C Your friends' home.

The worst thing that could happen to you would be:
- A To be seen walking naked around the house.
- B To have a confidence betrayed by a friend.
- C To be kept in the dark.

You would be most likely to knock on your neighbour's door:
- A If hell froze over.
- B If they made too much noise.
- C If you needed to borrow something.

As a teenager, you regarded your parents as:
- A A source of financial support.
- B A source of emotional support.
- C Friends.

If you have scored 0 to 13 points

You'd better watch out – you might overhear someone at work describing you as a miserable so-and-so. You can just about bring yourself to say 'Good morning' and you often leave at night without saying 'Goodbye'. You don't smile readily, let alone laugh. When people first meet you, they immediately class you as a cold fish. Admittedly, sometimes you just prefer to be alone but you don't ever take kindly to being interrupted while you're working or thinking.

You prefer closed spaces (you would hate to work in an office with a view) and solitary activities (you like playing patience, doing crosswords, reading, writing). Your idea of a group is two people. Three really is a crowd. The suggestion of an outing or a holiday with friends brings back bad memories of holiday camps. Sunday dinners with all the family ruin your weekend and Christmas is a nightmare. However, a lot of this could just be shyness. You would probably love to be less of a boor, make contact with people more easily, but you don't think you are capable of it. You prefer to stay on the sidelines because you are scared of being judged unfavourably.

But if people do regard you in an unsympathetic light, it's probably only because you usually do appear to be so cold and detached. If you could just try to show a little warmth and enthusiasm, things could turn out to be rather different ...

If you have scored 14 to 27 points

You are quite sociable on the whole. Of course, everyone has their bad moods and you sometimes disappear under your duvet in a huff. But, most of the time, you do appreciate the company of your friends and colleagues.

You find it easy to get on with people. Socially, you know by instinct when you can be brutally honest and when it's safer to tell a white lie. When you arrive at a party, you smile a lot (especially when you don't know anyone), and try to put everyone at their ease. You get nervous when you have to speak in public, but you manage it, even if you do mumble a little at first. Generally, you are quite spontaneous. You are not a real live wire but you enjoy going out in a group, to parties, to supper with friends or to big family dinners (even if your mother-in-law is there). You like to keep open house. You don't mind (at least not much) when friends or family turn up unexpectedly – you certainly prefer that to the sad alternative of being left munching on a sandwich on your own. Solitary pursuits are not your style. You need to share – and you do.

If you have scored 28 to 40 points
You are sociable to such a degree that it is almost pathological (especially if your score is closer to 40). You are of the stuff that disc-jockeys, Club Med organisers, pub singers and politicians are made of. Your idea of heaven is mingling with the crowd. You love shaking hands and kissing people on the cheeks (even when you don't know them) and you put the same enthusiasm into hugging your oldest friend and someone you've known 30 seconds. You are hyperdemonstrative, you need to please and to seduce (especially physically).

Equally, you are uncomfortable if you feel that nobody is paying attention to you. Some of this is down to exhibitionism, but a lot of it stems from your need to live within a group, be part of a team. You tend to panic about one-to-one relationships and when you are in a relationship with someone, you probably take them out a lot, to avoid being alone together as much as possible.

So calm down, relax – and stop trying so hard to be a party animal. If you could bear to let someone get to know the real individual that is you, instead of constantly presenting that madcap caricature of the person you think you should be, you might find you enjoy the experience more than you had expected.

ARE YOU AMBITIOUS?

SCORE:
2 points for each A answer
1 point for each B answer
0 points for each C answer

Add up the totals and look up the profile that corresponds to your score on pages 48–9.

You often have the feeling that you:
A Are dogged by ill luck.
B Were born under a lucky star.
C Deserve the good things in life.

At work, you most envy your friends':
A Job security.
B Future prospects.
C Success.

Being in a physical relationship with someone means:
A You have to reassure them.
B You have nothing to prove.
C You have nothing to learn.

You have problems:
A Getting up early.
B Getting off to sleep.
C Having a lie-in.

In primary school, you were:
A Pretty average.
B Often in the top five.
C Sometimes top.

In your job, your priority is to:
- A Get greater recognition for your work and your good points.
- B Get the chance to go on a course.
- C Get promoted.

Still at work, you would most like to change:
- A Your boss.
- B Your colleagues.
- C Your career.

When you think about your personal life, you feel that:
- A You are not quite normal.
- B You have the same problems as everyone else.
- C Your problems are unique.

Compliments and surprise gifts tend to:
- A Embarrass you.
- B Delight you.
- C Disappoint you.

You wish you could change:
- A Your first name.
- B Your family.
- C Your appearance.

When you were a teenager, your parents:
- A Didn't trust you very much.
- B Weren't always around.
- C Didn't listen to you enough.

When buying clothes, the first thing you look for is:
- A The price.
- B The quality.
- C The label.

You are sure that at work:
- A You are more efficient than others realise.
- B You are appreciated for what you are worth.
- C You deserve better than your present job.

If a friend managed to pull off a good deal, you would:
    A   Think they were lucky.
    B   Feel happy for them.
    C   Feel a little jealous.

Your mother-in-law obviously thinks you are a waste of space. You:
    A   Feel ashamed.
    B   Think she's being unfair.
    C   Get really angry.

Your partners in your erotic dreams are most likely to:
    A   Have no face.
    B   Be people you know.
    C   Be film stars or pop idols.

If your partner's mum arrives in town unexpectedly and he cancels your weekend together, you are most likely to feel:
    A   Not surprised – you weren't counting on it in any case.
    B   Not too put out – he's bound to find a moment for you too.
    C   Resentful.

In your opinion, the real key to success is:
    A   Money.
    B   Qualifications.
    C   Connections.

Asked to name your heart's desire, you would be most likely to say to the man in your life:
    A   'I don't want to lose you.'
    B   'I want to hold on to you.'
    C   'I want everything!'

The phrase that most closely describes your attitude to life is:
    A   'Things could be worse.'
    B   'I've always been lucky.'
    C   'I've still got so much to do.'

If you have scored 0 to 13 points

Your ambitions are rather modest, possibly even non-existent. Perhaps it's because your ego doesn't need to be flattered. You are happy with your lot – you quite like your life, your loves and your work and you can't really think how it could be made any better. Your dreams have (almost) all come true. You no longer aspire to anything special and your only ambition now is to steer clear of problems. That's fine.

But it may be that you have resigned yourself to your lack of success, power or glory. You may be so full of feelings of inferiority, you never truly believe that you could have personal or social success. Perhaps it's an achievement in itself that you get up every day and cope with all your problems. You rarely hope for anything better. And that's a real shame, because to be successful in work or love you need to have faith in yourself. To be able to change something, you need to believe very strongly that you can. Maybe you've stopped believing in yourself. Maybe you used to have big dreams, you were going to be a resounding success. But your decisions haven't always been the wisest or the best, and at times you've been dogged by sheer bad luck. Life has dealt you some hard knocks, but that's no reason to throw in the towel! Perhaps you should review your desires and your demands – you don't have to give up on yourself. You could still be a success if you just believe it's possible.

If you have scored 14 to 27 points

You are ambitious but you don't really go all-out for things. You want a lot, you sometimes think big, but you don't aim for the stars. You wouldn't dream of becoming a top model or basketball champion if you were somewhat challenged in the height department. You wouldn't aspire to a career as an international jetsetter if you feel sick just at the sight of a plane.

You are one of those people who simply don't believe that good luck will just drop into your lap. You believe in luck, of course, and you would seize every chance to turn good fortune to your advantage, but what you really believe is that we have to help the stars to smile on us – we are all in charge of our own destiny. The fantasy of unlimited success does not obsess you, and you are not convinced of your own great importance. You have a realistic view of your own abilities and you certainly don't regard yourself as the screw of the century just because you have multiple orgasms. Self-delusion, conceit or pretence are not in your make-up. You set yourself realistic objectives especially when you know a course of action is fraught with problems. You know how to pace yourself, you take as long as it takes. Both at work and in love, you know how to find a way to succeed.

If you have scored 28 to 40 points
You would do almost anything to achieve what you want because your insatiable appetite to reach the top drives you on. Socially, you have no doubts about your progress and no qualms about your behaviour. At work, you see no obstacles in your way and you think that success is your right. Result: you often succeed where others wouldn't even try.

You get quite a lot through nerve and bare-faced cheek. For you, the important thing is that you have self-belief. It certainly seems to work for you – just three months' training in anything from snowboarding to multimedia and you can pass as a pro. But you are sometimes very unrealistic: you get carried away with your dreams, when you would be better putting your efforts into your actual job or your relationship. It doesn't help that you go round whingeing that you have special problems which mean that only other exceptional people can understand you. You expect to receive preferential treatment for no good reason, and you take things badly if you are passed over in favour of someone else at work, or not automatically given the best table in a restaurant. If you don't get what you think you deserve, it makes you envious or jealous. You find it hard to stomach other people's success.

Don't let this resentment sour your outlook on life – you have such strength of character, you should not find it hard to remain optimistic. And just because others get to the top first, it doesn't mean that you can't join them.

ARE YOU ASSERTIVE?

SCORE:
2 points for each A answer
1 point for each B answer
0 points for each C answer

Add up the totals and look up the profile that corresponds to your score on pages 53–5.

The last time you changed jobs it was because:
A You were sacked.
B You found something better.
C You resigned on a whim.

You left home when you were:
A In your late twenties.
B Somewhere between the ages of 20 and 25.
C Still in your teens.

If, at a dinner party, you fall for a man who is clearly with someone:
A You don't even think about it, it's too complicated.
B You find a way of slipping him your telephone number.
C You let everyone know you have fallen under his spell.

When you are ill:
A It takes you a while to recover.
B You get better quickly.
C You are hardly ever ill.

If you had to help your child to choose a sport, you would encourage him/her to take up:
A Football.
B Tennis.
C Judo.

When you are going through serious emotional or practical problems, you:
- A Can't sleep.
- B Wake up every couple of hours all through the night.
- C Wake up very early in the morning.

When you were a child, your mother often used to say:
- A 'At least give it a try.'
- B 'Do your best.'
- C 'You can do better than that!'

When your boss has a fit and bawls you out, you:
- A Just stand there and take it.
- B Leave the room until he calms down.
- C Give as good as you get.

If your partner announced that he had met someone else, you would most likely:
- A Refuse to believe him, it can only be a passing fancy.
- B Tell him to pack up and go.
- C Take your revenge in his best friend's arms.

You have decided without thinking to have a go at parachuting, but at 10,000 feet you get the jitters. You:
- A Pull out – to hell with the shame.
- B Close your eyes and ask someone to push you.
- C Go for it – and tell yourself it will be easier next time.

The best way to solve your money problems would be to:
- A Marry into money.
- B Live less expensively.
- C Win the Lottery.

If your marks fall from your usual A+ to an A– you are most likely to think:
- A It shows just how bad you really are.
- B It doesn't matter, you can't always be top of the class.
- C It's just a blip, you'll be back to A+ next time.

You are most likely to use your holidays to:
- A Forget your worries.
- B Practise your favourite sport.
- C Look for a more interesting job.

If your partner says that you look like death warmed up, you are most likely to tell him:
- A You didn't get any sleep because you had a toothache.
- B You spent a night of passion with someone else (it's a big lie).
- C He's no oil painting himself.

You are getting married in two weeks. You are most likely to:
- A Begin to wonder if it's a really good idea.
- B Lose sleep, planning the day.
- C Do your best not to think about it.

In the jungle, in order to survive, you would eat:
- A Larvae and insects.
- B Raw toad or rat.
- C Human flesh.

In your opinion a successful team is one that:
- A Can work together accepting everybody's differences.
- B Can overcome its internal conflicts.
- C Encourages internal competition.

You hate a handshake that is:
- A Too strong.
- B Too weak.
- C Not a handshake at all – only the fingertips touch.

Success most often makes you feel:
- A Slightly guilty.
- B A little depressed.
- C Positively euphoric.

Faced with something you don't want to do, you are most likely to:
- A   Put it off until tomorrow.
- B   Try to pass it on to someone else.
- C   Rush through it to get it out of the way.

If you have scored 0 to 13 points
You are about as aggressive as a turnip. Your fighting spirit is apparently completely non-existent. You always go for the easy way out of things and you give up when faced with a difficulty. You like to do things the same way every day and you don't take risks.

You are set in your ways, you don't like change, and you hate any kind of new idea or suggestion. If you are out of sight of your familiar surroundings you feel lost and insecure. All kinds of obstacles and complications occur in your imagination. You often cancel plans at the last minute: you think it will rain on your picnic, your weekend will be ruined by traffic jams, the party will be spoilt because you are bound to say something stupid, your date will be a disaster because he won't like what you're wearing ...

At work, as in your relationships, you tend to make a drama out every little setback and panic in critical situations. Faced with the slightest obstacle, you are more likely to give up immediately than take any positive action. So you lose that promotion you were expecting, or that man you liked – everything passes you by. Of course, you would want to hold on to your loved one if you thought you were losing him. But even then, you wouldn't really fight for him – you just wouldn't believe you could win him back.

If you are going to have any success or happiness in your life, you are going to have to do something about your lack of self-belief. That is what is holding you back, and nothing else. So don't give up on something before you've begun just because it's unfamiliar to you – just tell yourself you can at least give it a try. And suddenly, you'll find most things aren't impossible after all.

If you have scored 14 to 27 points

You have an aggressive attitude to life. You are very dynamic, very focused and especially well-equipped for competition in your love life. Of course, like everyone else, you do get depressed, you have doubts about yourself and you sometimes feel over-stressed. But you have plenty of energy and will-power so nothing ever gets you down for long.

You bounce back pretty quickly after any sort of strain or failure or even a broken heart. If they show you the door, you come back in through the window. You don't see yourself being unemployed for too long. If your partner leaves you, you don't waste any time crying over it. You're not the type to brood or dwell on what might have been and you're not for ever looking for someone else to blame for your problems. As far as you are concerned, it's normal for things to go wrong, and when you do have mishaps it just means you can bounce back, probably with even more energy than before.

You see every problem as a challenge and the bigger the obstacle, the greater your motivation. You also know how best to use your fighting spirit: when you have an objective in your sights, you know instinctively whether you should go for it immediately or withdraw temporarily until the time is right.

If you have scored 28 to 40 points

You are not one to hide, bury your head in the sand or get under the table as soon as a problem shows up. Quite the opposite, in fact. You are happiest being the one who is up at the front, taking risks and you are at your best in a crisis.

On the surface you look tough, apparently capable of surviving in a hostile environment. And it's true, you can put up with a lot. But you tend to push your luck too much. You are always playing with fire and you tend to live on your nerves. You spend too much time in a state of emergency or stress. So what looks like aggression often turns out to be more of headlong rush into things. It's exhausting for you and for those around you.

At work, and in your relationships, the atmosphere is often one of tension, with some sort of conflict always lying just under the surface. You often pick a row with your partner when you are really angry with your boss (or vice versa). There is plenty of fight in you, but you try to take on too many battles at once, you are too ready to explode for no reason, and you often overreact – you get the big guns out when it really isn't necessary. Result: you make mistakes, you miss your targets and you end up failing to fulfil your objectives.

You tend to regard life as a series of battles that you have to fight. If you could resist getting involved in every skirmish, you would probably be pleasantly surprised at how many of them resolve themselves. Life will be a lot less stressful for you – and your friends and family!

DISCOVER YOUR EMOTIONAL PSYCHOSTYLE

Add up all your scores from the first four tests (see pages 10–33) and write the total on the horizontal line on the table below.

Next, add up all your scores from the second four tests (see pages 34–55) and write that total on the vertical line.

Draw a line between these two results. This will show which quadrant 'shapes' your personality.

For example: if you scored 91 points in tests the first four tests and 108 in the second four, you are an extrovert-impulsive.

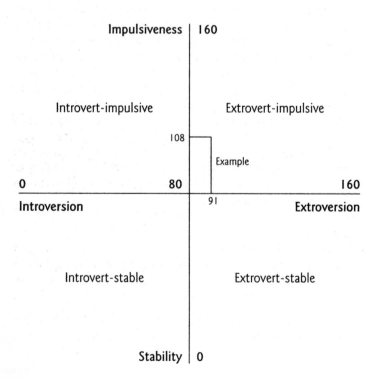

Extrovert-impulsive

You love new trends and technological advances (you adore surfing the Net); you're not too concerned with moral values, you hunger for sensation, excitement, new experiences and success. You take each day as it comes. Your motto in life is 'Every man for himself'.

You aim to sort out your financial affairs by taking advantage of any opportunities that present themselves. You crave social success – money is a great motivator for you – but you want to stay free and independent. Whether you work in a multinational, as part of a small team, or as a freelance individual, you prefer to remain detached. You do a good, professional job but you don't really get involved in your work or work for the joy of it. Added to which, as far as you're concerned, nothing lasts for ever and you have no intention of taking root.

You don't like to rest on your laurels either. Life for you is all about being out there, changing, discovering and moving things forward. You are hedonistic, you want to make the most of everything life has to offer, through your interests, your friends and, of course, sex. Outdoor pursuits take up a lot of your time. As far as you're concerned, home is strictly for sleeping in. Whatever you're looking for, whether it's culture or casual sex, you go out for it. You regularly work out to keep fit and you like experiencing physical activities and sensations, from feeling the burn in the gym to jetskiing in the surf. You live an active life: you take short holiday breaks all year round and enjoy trips abroad. However, you rarely go back to the same spot. You have a strong need for new pleasures and ever-changing experiences.

Extrovert-stable

You are generally opposed to change, and you have a somewhat withdrawn attitude to life. A private sort of person, perhaps this is because you are scared of the outside world or maybe because you are afraid of what the future may hold.

Traditional family values are important to you, and deep down you think a woman's place is in the home. Your family circle is more important to you than your work, and you would rather be nest-building than out there competing in the rat-race. You are the type to go home for lunch every day, and you wouldn't dream of working 18 hours at a stretch or over the weekend. First and foremost, you look for a quiet life, well-organised if at all possible, and you hate having your routine disturbed.

You are cautious, you prefer safe bets to risks. You are highly organised both at work and in your leisure pursuits. You enjoy routine jobs and taking breaks with your family. You are quite happy to go back to the same place for your holidays every year. You rarely travel long distances – it puts you in a bad mood. You have problems adapting to different ways of thinking, or changing your diet. Your traditions and principles are rock-solid and you tend to be quite singled-minded. Inclined to be rigid in your outlook, your strict moral and intellectual attitudes can border on the fanatical.

You prefer not to reveal too much of yourself and you function best in a very closed environment, amongst friends. You reject everything 'foreign' quite systematically and at times aggressively. You have rather old-fashioned views, and you veto everything that you think is too technological, newfangled or trendy.

Introvert-impulsive
You love all that is natural and unsophisticated and are very much against any sort of sham or pretence. You loathe all-out show and ostentation, and excessive displays of success and wealth. You yourself generally have little personal drive and you don't have a lot of aggression either, unless it's a question of defending someone's rights or fighting for a cause which you consider to be worthwhile.

When it comes to fashion or food, your tastes are simple. Your ideal would be to live with nature (you may be a bit of a trendy environmentalist) and to take your pleasure from simple things, escaping pressures and responsibilities as much as possible. You live from one day to the next. You find it difficult to organise yourself, you're not good at sticking to habits, or following a routine. You are easily distracted by your own mood swings.

Change and novelty are what you crave and you are insatiably curious. You are not much of a homebody and you certainly don't do much around the house. You dream of doing something adventurous (sexual or otherwise!) and escaping to foreign parts (sunbathing in Bali or trekking along the Grand Canyon). Most of all you would like to break away from your day-to-day routine.

Introvert-stable

You have high moral values and you are very attached to your principles and convictions. You believe that you have a duty to yourself and your family first and foremost.

Your life is divided between your family and your career. You are very centred, almost a little too much so, on your family, their physical and emotional comfort, the children's education and so on. And at the same time, you are passionate about your career. Privately and socially, you are, above all, discreet. You don't like to stand out and you have a taste for beautiful, understated clothes. You buy quality names. However, your desire to conform may also occasionally make you voice rather repressive moral views.

Anything new and groundbreaking tends to be viewed with mistrust, whether it is to do with technology or culture. Everything – people, objects, ideas – must have been tried and tested before they can receive your seal of approval. When you do commit yourself to something, it must have lasting worth.

You vote Tory, you prefer traditional decor (with some modern fittings of course) and you enjoy home cooking. For relaxation, you take holidays in the country (nothing too exotic, you like everything to be neat and tidy). You enjoy a little sailing, the odd round of golf, browsing in museums and visiting places of interest. Apart from that, you like watching television, reading books (especially historical novels), doing a little practical DIY around the house and collecting antiques.

You can be hard to please and your exacting tastes may put a strain on your friendships. Your social life tends to revolve around the private clubs and associations you belong to.

PART 2

WHAT SORT OF A WOMAN ARE YOU?

ARE YOU STILL A WOMAN?

The majority of women, we know, naturally have a higher EQ than men – it is a part of their feminine character. But every woman also has masculine aspects to her character, to a greater or lesser extent, which will affect the level of her EQ. Added to this, it now seems that the independence and equality women fought so hard to gain in the twentieth century may have cost them a little of their emotional intelligence. The following test will help you to evaluate the different mental, emotional and sexual levels of your feminine and masculine aspects.

As before, always choose the answer that most closely matches your own likely response and add up the totals.

SCORE:
Add up the numbers of ✳ ○ ❖ ❑ ▼ ✺ and read the profiles that correspond to your scores on pages 66–9.

Your ability to remain faithful is severely tested when:
- ▼ You meet an attractive, sexy man.
- ❑ You have an argument with your partner.
- ✳ You feel sexually frustrated.
- ❖ A man makes it clear he wants you very badly.

To be with the man you love, you would be prepared to:
- ❖ Live less comfortably.
- ❑ Go to live abroad.
- ✳ Completely change the way you look.
- ✳ Risk your life.

You are broke. To feed your children, you would:
- ✳ Work as a cleaner.
- ▼ Become a prostitute.
- ❑ Work as a gardener.
- ○ Rob a bank.

Your best friend drives you up the wall when she:
- ▼ Won't tell you all about her latest night of passion.
- ❑ Moans about everything.
- ○ Loses all her common sense because she's in love.
- ✳ Betrays your confidence.

You are quite happy to:
- ○ Share the bill with a man in a restaurant.
- ❖ Have a wee in front of your partner.
- ▼ Use your charms to get what you want at work.
- ❑ Shop for underwear with your boyfriend in tow.

When you are out with your man, you walk:
- ○ Slightly ahead of him.
- ✳ Slightly behind him.
- ❖ On his left.
- ❑ On his right.

It really annoys you when your partner:
- ❏ Lies to you.
- ❖ Gets out of doing the housework – again.
- ✳ Says 'I told you so'.
- ✺ Insists on making love when you don't feel like it.

A home is not complete without:
- ▼ Lots of houseplants.
- ✺ A reinforced door.
- ◯ A fax machine.
- ❖ Family photos on the walls.

You wish your partner:
- ▼ Was a bit more affectionate.
- ❏ Spent more time looking after the children.
- ✺ Used more imagination in bed.
- ✳ Helped more with the housework.

You would be most upset if you had to give up:
- ✳ Your career.
- ✺ The possibility of having children.
- ❖ Most of your money.
- ❏ Living with someone.

If you were having an affair, you would be found out because:
- ❖ You would keep buying new underwear.
- ✳ You would come home at night freshly made-up.
- ◯ You would be more aggressive towards your partner.
- ✺ You would be all over him.

You most dread:
- ▼ Going to the dentist.
- ◯ Losing your job.
- ✳ Walking home alone late at night.
- ✺ Being a sexual failure.

In your favourite fantasy you are most likely to be:
- ✺ Being caressed whilst you're driving.
- ▼ Being taken by force by several men.
- ○ Making love with a nun.
- ✳ Being tied up by a very hairy man.

Your watch:
- ○ Is indispensable.
- ❖ Is something you often forget to put on.
- ✺ Stays on even when you make love.
- ▼ Is taken off before you go to sleep.

The sexiest invention of the last 30 years is:
- ✺ The G-string.
- ▼ The miniskirt.
- ❏ Hold-ups.
- ❖ The Wonderbra.

You often:
- ○ Read the newspaper at the table.
- ❏ Go to a café.
- ❖ Cook with fresh ingredients.
- ▼ Invite a man you like to dinner.

If you could have a penis for 24 hours, you would like to try:
- ✳ Weeing standing up.
- ▼ Making love to a woman.
- ✺ Making love to a man.
- ○ Masturbating.

You feel most healthy:
- ▼ In summer.
- ✺ In autumn.
- ✳ In winter.
- ❏ In spring.

If you wanted to kill yourself, you would:
- ✳ Cut your wrists.
- ❖ Drink poison.
- ❏ Hang yourself.
- ◯ Shoot yourself in the head.

If a colleague at work pinched your bottom, you would:
- ✺ Slap him hard.
- ❖ Ignore it – but only once.
- ▼ Report him to your boss.
- ◯ Make sure you don't turn your back to him from now on.

You have always felt closest to your:
- ✺ Paternal grandfather.
- ◯ Maternal grandfather.
- ❖ Paternal grandmother.
- ▼ Maternal grandmother.

You would find it most difficult to:
- ✳ Read a map.
- ❏ Write a love letter.
- ▼ Let a man know you want him.
- ✺ Do a strip-tease.

If a man doesn't try to kiss you on your first date; you think:
- ▼ 'He doesn't like me.'
- ❏ 'He's very shy.'
- ◯ 'He has sexual hang-ups.'
- ❖ 'He's in love.'

You find that male models are quite:
- ❖ Natural.
- ✳ Inaccessible.
- ❏ Annoying.
- ◯ Pretentious.

It is very important to you that your partner:

* ✳ Really listens to you.
* ❏ Encourages you to reach your goals.
* ❖ Takes notice of your appearance.
* ○ Shares your problems.

More ✳ than ○

There's no doubt about it – you think like a woman. The right side of your brain is dominant and that's the side that prefers to gossip about clothes rather than discuss a balance sheet, and appreciates the curve of a nice bum rather than the lines of a sales graph.

You can't find your way round with a simple town map, and you couldn't even begin to calculate the price of things in euro. You can't understand the weather forecast unless the temperatures are in Fahrenheit, and when it comes to time, you have the sort of internal clock which is unique to women: 'Just one more minute' means ten (at least) and 'I'll be ready in ten minutes' means a good hour. You can transform the look of a room with just a few cushions and candlesticks but it would take you all day to work out how to change a plug.

Most feminine of all, you can think about several things at once. You can make the week's shopping list and plan the week's meals whilst taking the minutes at a very important meeting and still remember to call your man when you come out.

More ○ than ✳

You think more like a man. Men are controlled by the left side of their brain and, like them, you are more at ease programming your video than the washing machine. You can change a wheel but half the time you can't remember where you parked your car. You are always looking for your keys, or your underwear.

And yet you can be very meticulous about small things: it drives you up the wall when your partner leaves the top off the toothpaste tube, the peanut butter jar or your moisturiser (which he's borrowed). You are the same at work: you can spend hours analysing a file but you don't have five minutes for your PA who's feeling oversensitive right now and could do with a shoulder to cry on. You can also be quite cutting when you feel it's necessary and you're certainly not scared of confrontation with any of your male colleagues.

More ❖ than ❑
You love like a woman. You can still cry buckets when you are watching *Dr Zhivago* on TV for the umpteenth time, and at work you break down if your boss reprimands you for having missed a client presentation (it's just not fair – it was a lousy product anyway). You can even cry for no reason at all. You are far better at explaining to one of the guys at work what you think of his new girlfriend (she's no good for him) than at discussing the effects of the latest budget with your partner.

You believe in true love – of course. So you are equally sure, every time you fall in love, that there is only one man for you and this time, it really is him. When there's a man in your life, you can behave like a complete fool. You are enraptured by his every exploit (he came 9,243rd in the New York marathon). You take everything he says as gospel ('Tomorrow I'll tell her all about us, she can keep the house and the children, but it's you I want' or 'Don't worry about that little blonde at the office, she's just an old friend'). And you just love lying awake, listening to him snore.

More ❑ than ❖
You have something of a masculine side to you although you are still very much a woman. So, like most women, you get in a state when you are in love. (You lose your appetite, you drop things a lot, you dial his number by mistake when you're trying to ring your mother.) And you never fail to surprise him for his birthday, you write to tell him you love him on Valentine's Day, you know how to wrap your arms round when he has a bad case of the blues.

But at the same time, you feel that there is no reason for him to think that he owns you or expect you to behave like his mother. You have your own problems and you need to have your own life too.

You need space to breathe and, as far as you're concerned, you should be allowed to go out with your own friends – or even your ex – if you want to.

More ▼ than ❋

When it comes to love, you are definitely very much a woman. You tend to lower your gaze when you find yourself fancying someone. You blush easily, you constantly run your hand through your hair, you bite your lips – and it all drives the men wild because it's all part of the body language that says you are attracted to them. Of course, the person sitting opposite you has to be able to read the signs and he'll need to understand that if you don't let him kiss you on your first date, it's actually rather a good sign.

He'll also have to know that what you like most about sex is that loving feeling. You need to be emotionally involved before you'll want to start anything, otherwise there's no satisfaction in it for you. If there's no tenderness in a relationship, you'd rather stick to eating chocolate – it's a lot less likely to get you hurt. In bed, you tend to be rather passive. You prefer to lie back and let your partner lead the love dance. And you don't need a performance worthy of Casanova to satisfy you – your happiness comes from within you, it's an emotional, not a physical, reaction.

More ❋ than ▼

When it comes to love, you behave rather more like a man. You enjoy sexual adventures, and fidelity is not really terribly important to you. The smallest physical detail can arouse you, such as the delicious strength of a man's jaw, the set of his shoulders, the way you can imagine his hands moving over your ... You don't need to be wooed to get into bed with someone – you just do it because you feel like it.

You may make love out of curiosity, or for the pure physical pleasure of it or because the fact that you haven't had it for three days is beginning to bother you. When you fancy a man, you don't hang around waiting for him to make the first move and you certainly don't expect to be wined and dined for weeks before you let him ruffle your underwear. It's more likely to be 'Your place or mine' from the first night.

Of course, you hate being turned down and your constant pestering may end up annoying your partner, especially if he would rather be exploring the Net than your body. In bed, you lead (you'd rather be on top than underneath) and you're not interested in long-drawn-out sessions of foreplay. Satisfaction is what you're after, and the sooner the better.

ARE YOU A MOTHER-FIGURE OR A BIT OF A TART?

There are some women with whom men want to make babies and there are those with whom they want to make love. At times it can be the same person. The way you and your man react to each other, day and night, tells you what he thinks of you, and how his feelings influence your relationship. The following questions will help you to discover what sort of woman you are to him.

Look at each statement and decide which response is closest to your own. Write down all your As, Bs, Cs and Ds.

SCORE:
Add up the numbers of As, Bs, Cs and Ds you score, then look at the corresponding assessments on pages 74–6. If you have less than two points difference between two totals, read both the relevant assessments. You have characteristics of both.

You often:
- A Buy his underpants.
- B Make his dinner.
- C Get him a drink.
- D Wash his socks.

He announces that he'll be having Christmas Eve dinner with his ex and his kids, so you suggest:
- A That he rejoins you however late it is.
- B That he has dinner on Christmas Day with you.
- C That he spends the whole of New Year's Eve with you.
- D That you might just spend the night with someone else.

If you told him you had fallen for someone else, he would:
A Go crazy.
B Run off with the children.
C Think it's just your hormones playing up temporarily.
D Give you an ultimatum: 'That bastard or me.'

After making love, he likes to:
A Talk.
B Go to sleep.
C Be alone.
D Start again.

After a week of lazing on a Spanish beach with you, your partner suddenly announces that he's bored and he's going off for a few days to see a local bull-fighting festival. You:
A Beg him to take you with him, you love that sort of thing.
B Fly home without him and wait for him to come back.
C Take the opportunity to get off with the local diving instructor.
D Follow him to see what he's really doing – and with whom.

When you were in your teens:
A Your parents never minded you going out alone at night.
B Your mother knew you used to sneak out – and she let you.
C Your mother used to stop you going out.
D You liked staying in.

If your best friend's husband told you he suspected she'd got someone else, you would:
A Accuse him of neglecting her too much.
B Convince him that it was all in his mind.
C Offer to help him get over it.
D Drop her in it by telling him everything you know.

When you are in a relationship, you hate:
    A Having to be apart.
    B Breaking up.
    C The loss of your privacy.
    D Having to be considerate.

A so-called friend telephones you to tell you that she has just seen your man with someone else. You tell her:
    A 'You always think the worst of everyone.'
    B 'I don't want to know.'
    C 'It must be his wife.'
    D 'Tell me more.'

He refuses to leave his wife and three children and move in with you. You think this means:
    A He doesn't really love you.
    B He needs more time.
    C It's probably better this way after all.
    D He's a cowardly jerk.

The saddest thing about your relationship is that:
    A He's less attentive than he was in the beginning.
    B He's wonderful in public but sulks at home.
    C He's not romantic enough.
    D He never wants to make any plans for the future.

One of the best things about it is that he:
    A Often surprises you by taking you out to dinner.
    B Is happy with a meal out of a packet.
    C Brings you breakfast in bed.
    D Loves you for your body, not your cooking.

If you caught him in your best friend's arms, he would say:
    A It's because he was missing you terribly.
    B It happened in the heat of the moment, it was stupid and it'll never happen again.
    C He can do what he likes with his body.
    D You drove him to do it.

Your lover gets guilty if he thinks:
- A   He's putting on weight.
- B   He doesn't look after his children as much as he should.
- C   He has no time for you.
- D   He rarely has a guilty conscience.

It doesn't bother you that he:
- A   Snores.
- B   Rarely makes love to you.
- C   Wees in the sink.
- D   Is married.

If you accused him of lying to you and demanded the truth, you would expect him to:
- A   Still give you only half the story.
- B   Confess everything and promise it will never happen again.
- C   Deny everything, even though it means lying more.
- D   Slap you.

Your partner objects the most when you:
- A   Talk about your ex.
- B   Have lunch with your ex.
- C   Draw comparisons between him and your ex.
- D   Have dinner with your ex.

If you still weren't home by 4 o'clock in the morning, he would call:
- A   All the hospitals and police stations.
- B   Your mum.
- C   All the nightclubs.
- D   All your exes.

If you saw a man stealing a scarf in a shop, you would:
- A   Let him know that you saw him.
- B   Lecture him.
- C   Mind your own business.
- D   Point him out to a sales assistant.

Men tend to:
- A   Believe that you are entirely sincere.
- B   Indulge you even when they think you are wrong.
- C   Expect special treatment from you.
- D   Doubt your honesty.

The last time you made love:
- A   You both wanted to.
- B   Neither of you really felt like it.
- C   You really wanted to but he didn't.
- D   He really wanted to but you didn't.

Really falling in love:
- A   Is when two become one.
- B   Takes two.
- C   Can happen several times in a lifetime.
- D   Usually ends badly.

In order to pinch another woman's man, you would be prepared to:
- A   Give him the keys to your flat.
- B   Get pregnant without telling him.
- C   Become his sexual slave.
- D   Call his wife and tell her everything.

If he couldn't be your partner, you would want him to be:
- A   Your twin.
- B   Your father.
- C   Your bank manager.
- D   Your psychologist.

Highest total As

You really do offer two for the price of one. You are his idea of the perfect mother (he can see himself raising a family with you) and his perfect lover (he has no wish to go and see if the grass is greener anywhere else). In your arms, he can lead a double life; one moment he can be Mummy's little boy and the next he can fulfil all his sexual fantasies. Where could he ever find anything better?

So you can have it all: a relationship and a man who's crazy about you because you are can surprise and delight him with something new (well, almost) every day. You've got it made. He doesn't ever have a fit if the fridge is empty (he just takes you out to dinner) and he's very good about cleaning the bath after he's used it (he knows how much those hairs in the plughole upset you).

Highest total Bs
You are made to be a mother – as far as he's concerned. He will definitely marry you. He sees you first and foremost as his wife, the one who will give him beautiful babies (preferably boys) and who will take good care of them. The advantage is that you have a guaranteed place in his life, even if he's not exactly a well-proven monogamist. His little extramarital escapades won't threaten your relationship. He's not the type who will desert you and the children for a passing bit of skirt. At least, not in the first few years.

Later, however, as the children grow up, with his mid-life crisis approaching, he may become rather more unstable. You would do well to remember that in the long term it's a mistake to settle for just playing the perfect wife. You stand a better chance of keeping your man if you can become his mistress once again too.

Highest total Cs
He sees you as his mistress, no doubt about it. He entertains you, he always wants you, he never gets tired of you. He whisks you off to lunch, for a weekend in the sun, a holiday on a faraway island. He is wonderfully attentive and really appreciates you. Best of all, you only ever see the good side of him. He doesn't bore you with tales of his office politics and he (almost) never bothers you with his personal problems. Added to which, he doesn't want to poke his nose into your affairs too much either. He rarely interferes and doesn't want to know how you use your time.

Your relationship with him is certainly very stable and comfortable, but the downside is that it is rather detached. This means that the day he decides to have children, he'll probably want to have them with someone else; and if he already has them, he's happy with things as they are. You are cast in your role and it can't be changed. He can't imagine you making baby talk (well, not to a baby) or being up to your eyes in nappies and bottles. The only way to make sure that he doesn't chuck you for a baby-maker – which means you will only ever be second best – is to show him you can and will share bad times with him as well as good.

Highest total Ds
You're not quite the type to be his wife, and you're not really a mistress; he doesn't know how to see you. At any moment, you could be something of an inconvenience to him. He doesn't think that he would enjoy living with you long-term (even if you did buy the duvet together). When he looks to you for anything (which isn't often), he doesn't see you as someone to give him support, he just wants to moan about his problems (which are always the same) or his needs (which are always urgent).

You can never get it right with him. At best, you are an occasional source of passing pleasure before he goes back to more serious matters: the chap at the office who's giving him problems, his wife who doesn't understand him (he's usually married), his kids who all have asthma, etc. And at worst, you are his cleaning lady (he moans when you leave his dirty socks lying around). If you want to change things, you'll have to decide which role suits you best and go for it. Show him what sort of woman you are – mother or mistress – and how you want to be treated. If that doesn't work, the only other solution is to change your man.

ARE YOU THE PESTERING KIND?

A good EQ makes you more seductive. But there are many ways of seducing. Are you prepared to do anything, even the worst you can imagine, to get the man you want? Read the following statements, choose your most likely response and add up your scores as before to discover just how far you will go to get your man.

SCORE:
Add up the number of As, Bs and Cs you score, then look at the corresponding assessments on pages 80–2. You share the characteristics of two profiles if you have less than two points difference between them.

When you are in love, you:
    A Wait by the phone.
    B Call him several times a day.
    C Arrive unannounced at his place in the middle of the night.

You have been known to:
    A Turn and walk backwards to look at a man in the street.
    B Follow a man down the road.
    C Put your hand on a man's bum.

You have asked him out ten times and he's refused (politely) every time. You are most likely to:
    A Forget about him.
    B Ask him out just once more.
    C Wait for him outside his office.

If he says he's having a quiet night in at his own place, you:
    A Leave him to it.
    B Ring him several times during the night to check he's there.
    C Keep ringing and hanging up to make things tricky if he's with someone else.

You think that it's quite normal to:
  A   Call him just to hear his voice.
  B   Listen to the messages on his answering machine.
  C   Have a spare key to his flat cut without telling him.

He refuses to come with you for dinner with friends, so you:
  A   Leave him behind and call him the next day to tell him
      about the evening.
  B   Work on your friends to make them insist that he comes.
  C   Keep on at him until he changes his mind.

At a friend's dinner party, you find yourself seated opposite the most fanciable man you have seen in months. So you:
  A   Gaze at him all evening and hope they invite you together
      again next time.
  B   Arrange it so that he takes you home.
  C   Play footsie with him.

Sometimes men accuse you of being:
  A   Too preoccupied with your work.
  B   A bit too possessive.
  C   All over them like a rash.

In your fantasies, you often imagine:
  A   Making love to someone other than your partner.
  B   Making love to a woman.
  C   Having a sex slave.

Your father is the one person:
  A   You don't want the man in your life to resemble.
  B   You would like to know better.
  C   You don't think loved you very much.

You are not worried about coming on to someone:
  A   At a friend's house.
  B   On the Net.
  C   In the street.

After the first (great) passionate night, you are most likely to:
  A Sit and wait for him to call.
  B Leave a message on his answering machine telling him what a wonderful time you had.
  C Chase him up at work to talk about it.

If he stops calling you, you think it means:
  A 'He's had enough of me.'
  B 'He's worried about something and he doesn't dare tell me.'
  C 'He's waiting for me to call him.'

He screens his calls to avoid you. In response, you:
  A Cross his name off your agenda.
  B Write a six-page letter to tell him what you think of him.
  C Turn up at his office unannounced to ask for an explanation.

He chucks you. You:
  A Turn off your phone and go into hiding.
  B Leave a rose in his letterbox every day.
  C Camp on his doorstep.

You like to eat:
  A Little and often.
  B Hardly at all.
  C Everything in sight.

A man only gives flowers when he:
  A Is in love.
  B Is trying to win someone over.
  C Has done something wrong.

You find it best to:
  A Draw a veil over your past.
  B Ask a man about his past sex life.
  C Tell him about your past sex life.

When you're in love, there's nothing worse than being:
- A Deceived.
- B Betrayed.
- C Told that as far as he's concerned it's finished.

If he was in a relationship you wanted to break up, you would:
- A Wait patiently on the sidelines.
- B Give him the key to your home.
- C Tell his wife everything.

Highest total As

You are discreet, detached and you don't like hassling people. You have had to put up with enough misery from men who behaved like limpets and you don't want to behave like one yourself. You don't try to seduce a man by forcing yourself on him: it's not your style and anyway, it's against your principles. You think self-respect goes hand in hand with respect for other people. So before you go after a man, there must be mutual attraction. You want him to positively like you, not just give in because he's been worn down by you.

If you are interested in someone, you show it but you like them to do the same. You are happy to take the initiative, but you also need to get some sort of feedback and if the other person doesn't respond, you won't persist. You don't plan any sort of strategy; you need things to happen naturally, you like a bit of spontaneity in your relationships. You would never try to insinuate yourself, uninvited, into a man's heart or his life. You need to know that he shares your feelings of love and desire.

The more you love a man, the more discreet you become – you are almost too anxious not to crowd him. You wouldn't dream of poking your nose into his private life or his business affairs, unless he said you could. And when you do move into his life, you will do so with such tact and delicacy, he will hardly notice you've arrived.

Highest total Bs

You are so cunning, your forte is weaselling your way into a man's life. When you fancy a man, you are don't attack him from the front. Infiltration is more your pulling style. You have devised a whole series of crafty manoeuvres designed to make him fall into your charming trap, and sometimes you use them almost subconsciously.

You slip quite naturally into the heart – or the bed – of a man if you want him. After all, you like him. It would never occur to you that the feeling may not be mutual, or that he might just find you attractive and pleasant, without necessarily wanting to sleep with you (or at least without wanting to make a habit of it). You think it's a foregone conclusion that he will fall for your charms eventually, even if it takes some time. You have lots of little tricks up your sleeve and you play your game of seduction with great patience.

You can also be very clever and calculating. You don't move straight in on him, you don't bombard him with phone calls, but little by little you somehow make yourself become an indispensable part of his life. You make sure there are plenty of 'chance' meetings between you and then you ask how he is, you invite him over to your flat at least once a week, for a pizza, to watch a video, to see your holiday snaps (topless, of course). If none of this works, you find other ways of insinuating yourself into his life. You volunteer to help him redecorate his flat, you organise meetings with people who can be useful to him socially or professionally, you make friends with his crowd to get yourself invited to the same dinners and parties. 'By coincidence', you join the same sports club. In short, you make yourself a familiar figure in his life. Plus, you make yourself available, always on hand when he needs someone.

Once he's hooked, you make sure he ends up depending on you, although you do give him the illusion of still being free. He'll never know how it happened, but now he doesn't even think about escaping those sweet clutches of yours.

Highest total Cs

You have all the grace and charm of a caveman. You think that if women are socially equal to men, why not sexually? Men can impose their will, you think, so why shouldn't you do the same? It doesn't occur to you that men dislike being 'taken' just as much as most women do; and somehow you hadn't realised that believing that persistence will always pay off ('They all give in eventually') is as unattractive in a woman as it is in a man.

When you want a man, it seems that you don't really care too much about what he wants, or how he feels. You try (and quite often succeed) in forcing your way through to what you want. With you in pursuit, there's no time to get to know each other. You will throw yourself quite readily into the arms – or the bed – of a virtual stranger. You refuse to accept that a man may be trying to put you off. If he's not interested, it must be because he has another woman, and so you start manoeuvring in a big way against the real or supposed rival. You call him several times every evening to keep him (and his answering machine) busy, hoping at the same time that it will provoke a row if he is with someone. You keep popping into his office to visit him at odd times, or you turn up unexpectedly in the middle of the night at his place. You try to corner him, literally; you want to own him, you will use your body to keep him with you (sad, isn't it?)

And then, when you have him, you're still not satisfied. You tend to be very possessive, and you may insist that he puts your needs before everything and everyone else. Try to curb your urges and be less demanding – you don't want to be a complete tyrant.

ARE YOU UNFORGETTABLE?

If you have a good EQ, people never forget you completely. So, once you have been with a man, are memories of you engraved indelibly on his mind? Or did you just flit like a temporary shadow across the landscape of his life? This test will give you the answers.

Look at the statements below and keep a score of your most likely responses to them.

> **SCORE:**
> Add up the numbers of As, Bs and Cs you score, then look at the corresponding assessments on pages 85–7. You share the characteristics of two profiles if you have less than two points' difference between them.

Usually, men tell you they are crazy about your:
- A Figure.
- B Voice.
- C Eyes.

You can feel sexually at ease with a man:
- A After a few months.
- B After a few days.
- C From the first night.

If your partner accused you of lying, you would:
- A Try to prove your innocence.
- B Take no notice, he says so many stupid things.
- C Slap him.

Most of your ex-boyfriends:
- A Have completely disappeared from your life.
- B Still occasionally get in touch with you.
- C Have become your friends.

If you bumped into an old boyfriend from about 15 years ago, he would probably say:

A 'Don't I know you from somewhere?'

B 'You smell just the same.'

C 'What are you doing tonight?'

When you flirt with a man:

A It can get a bit boring.

B There's often a strong sexual attraction.

C You are always very loving.

When it comes to ending affairs:

A You are most often the one who is given the big E.

B It's even Stephens – sometimes you are dumped, sometimes you do the dumping.

C You are almost always the one to finish it.

The last man you left:

A Disappeared – you've never seen him since.

B Still calls you with any excuse.

C Cried and said: 'I'll always be here if you want to come back ...'

Men in love will do all sorts of things to please. You once had a man who, just for you, managed to:

A Give up going clubbing every night.

B Stop smoking.

C Leave his wife.

On your birthday:

A You always know that at least your mum will phone.

B One of your exes will pop in.

C All your favourite exes call you.

In the past, you've had lots of men who:

A Said 'I'll call you' and never did.

B Asked you to live with them.

C Asked you to have their baby.

When you start a new relationship:
- A You adapt to his way of life.
- B You change the way he looks.
- C You make him change his lifestyle, his habits.

Quite often, a man you've seen two or three times tells you:
- A 'You remind me of someone I used to know.'
- B 'Last night I dreamt about you.'
- C 'I think we've known each other in another life.'

In your opinion, a man prefers living with a woman who is:
- A Wonderful in bed.
- B A cordon bleu cook.
- C Intelligent.

Your ideal house for a weekend of passionate love-making would be:
- A A water mill.
- B A house on stilts on a lake.
- C A house overlooking the sea.

Your swimming costume is:
- A An old one-piece you had for swimming at school.
- B High-leg bikini bottoms.
- C A bikini.

You would find it easy to make an unforgettable impression on:
- A Trevor McDonald.
- B Harrison Ford.
- C Brad Pitt.

Highest total As
You are rather easy to forget. Out of sight, out of mind ... As soon as you disappear from a man's field of vision, his arms or his life, you unfortunately tend to sink into oblivion. You've stopped counting the number of times you've given someone your phone number and waited in vain. You are one of those they just don't call at all, or so rarely it makes no difference.

Why? Sometimes it's because you don't choose your men well. But mostly, it's because even as a child you always had the habit of being utterly forgettable – you just blended in with the wallpaper. Now you're grown up, you are too polite and too discreet to leave your mark anywhere. By never making waves, by not making any fuss, you end up being part of the furniture. You are so well behaved, you don't make any impression on people's minds. If you don't want to be forgotten, you must learn to make more impact. You'll have to improve your image, as advertisers say.

So it's time to stop sliding into a man's life like a shadow. Start making more sensational entrances and exits, learn to make a song and dance. Take every opportunity to make people notice you. Go for a more sexy, more original look. Express your views more often (and with more conviction). Don't say yes to everything. And don't worry about overdoing it. Whatever you do, the important thing is to get noticed.

Highest total Bs

You are utterly memorable. No one ever forgets you, not really, never completely. You may lose touch with someone but you still don't disappear from their memory. You remain on their mind and in their heart despite the distance, the passage of time and the parting of the ways. The little kids you were with at primary school remember you and so do the lads you were at college with. You'd be surprised at the number of people who have fond memories of you, some for the good times you shared, others for the times they would have liked to have shared with you.

You make a huge impression. The men who've been seduced by you are always left thinking of what might have been. So it's hardly surprising if those you've loved still think about you several years later. Of course, not every day, that would be weird. But they think about you fairly regularly. Sometimes, they dream about you. They will suddenly find themselves reminded of you by a gesture, a perfume or a look in another woman. On your birthday at least two of your old boyfriends will always call you to wish you many happy returns. And every now and then, one of your ex-lovers turns up out of the blue to see you. It's a mystery how on earth they manage to find you after you've moved several times, even when you are ex-directory. Clearly, you must have left them with some amazingly good memories. And the reason is because when you give yourself, you do so completely; sometimes, as much in one night as others do in a whole life.

Highest total Cs

You are really charismatic, unforgettable like Garbo. Unfortunately, perhaps, too much so. Life is (almost) not worth living without you. And of course this sort of thing creates problems in your love life. You always have the greatest difficulty in making a man understand when it's over. They never seem to accept that it's completely finished, they can't wean themselves off you. They become obsessed and desperately try to hang on, before finally sinking into miserable resignation. Some may make themselves ill over you. Others become 'just good friends' so that they can maintain some kind of link and keep in contact with you. As a result, since you were a teenager you've accumulated an astonishing number of admirers who keep in touch and still send you flowers on Valentine's Day. It's all very flattering.

And it's all because you give yourself very rarely but when you do it's heart, body and soul. For you, a man always commits himself totally, definitely, exclusively, absolutely. In his eyes, you are the only woman in his life, the one he's been dreaming about, the one he's been waiting for for years. By coming into his life, even if it's for just one night, you don't just change his look, his way of life, his habits. You also mark him deeply and permanently. After you, he'll never be the same again. He will have known the greatest joys, but also the greatest suffering. No wonder he can't forget you.

ARE YOU HUNGRY FOR LOVE?

'Do you love me?' 'Yes I do.' 'Do you really love me?' 'Yes, I really love you.' 'But do you really, really love me?' 'Yes, I really, really love you.' 'Really, truly, really?' And so on ...

If you are too hungry for love, it ends up putting people off. They will quickly come to the conclusion that, no matter what they do, they can never make you happy. If you ask too much, people will avoid you.

If you are someone who's hungry for love, the affection you crave has the same effect as food does for a bulimic person, or drugs for an addict. It gives you a temporary lift, but it doesn't satisfy you. Suddenly, that's all you can think about. You have to have it and every fix has to be bigger than the one before. You are prepared to do anything to feel loved. You become capable of almost every kind of persuasive behaviour, even blackmail, to get what you want.

Of course, it's natural to want to be loved. Everyone needs love, especially when things are going badly. Some people undoubtedly need it more than others, for example those who were deprived of affection – or, conversely, overindulged – in their childhood.

It is possible to avoid an unhealthy craving for love and affection by developing your own emotional intelligence, and improving your relationships with other people. If you suspect you are too hungry for love, you have to identify first of all, the 'illness', the form it takes. Then, you need to strengthen your immune system to limit any damage during 'a crisis'.

So, how badly affected are you? Which of the following statements apply to you? Answer honestly, yes or no, then refer to the score panel on page 90 and the assessments on pages 91–5.

1   You constantly seek reassurance and approval from
    other people at work and in your private life.   Yes/No

2   You feel angry, ashamed or humiliated if someone
    criticises you (even slightly).   Yes/No

3   You are incapable of choosing a new dress without
    someone to help you.   Yes/No

4   You desperately want people to admire your
    appearance.   Yes/No

5   You think it's acceptable to use other people to
    get what you want.   Yes/No

6   Where you live is a matter of circumstances,
    not choice.   Yes/No

7   You would burst into tears if you heard that your
    best friend's dog had died.   Yes/No

8   You often overestimate your abilities or the value
    of your achievements.   Yes/No

9   You tend to agree too often with people, even when
    you think they are wrong.   Yes/No

10 At parties, you don't feel happy unless you are the
    centre of attention.   Yes/No

11 You think that only exceptional people can really
    understand your problems.   Yes/No

12 You would not feel capable of organising a solo
    holiday trip.   Yes/No

13 Your emotional reactions are not predictable.   Yes/No

14 You would really like being one of the world's
    top models.   Yes/No

15 If there's a horrible job to be done at work or
    at home, you always volunteer to do it.   Yes/No

16 When you want something, you want it
straight away.   Yes/No

17 You often jump queues.   Yes/No

18 You would go out to dinner with a man you don't
like very much to avoid being at home alone.   Yes/No

19 You are not good at describing an event or a person
in detail.   Yes/No

20 You fish for compliments a lot.   Yes/No

21 You feel devastated when a close relationship
is broken off.   Yes/No

22 You don't take it well when a friend cancels on you
even if it is not her fault.   Yes/No

23 You worry about the thought of someone
leaving you.   Yes/No

24 You frequently feel jealous or envious of your
friends' lives.   Yes/No

25 You are easily hurt by criticism from your partner.   Yes/No

26 You often wear miniskirts and figure-hugging
tops to the office.   Yes/No

SCORE:

You are NOT hungry for love if you answered NO to:

At least five of questions 1, 4, 7, 10, 13, 16, 19, 26.

Or

At least five of questions 2, 5, 8, 11, 14, 17, 20, 22, 24.

Or

At least five of questions 3, 6, 9, 12, 15, 18, 21, 23, 25.

If your score so far (see panel on page 90) shows that you ARE hungry for love, you will fall into one of three categories: histrionics; egocentrics; and 'orphans', who are afraid of being abandoned. Look at your scores again to see which category best describes you.

SCORE:
If you answered YES to at least four out of questions 1, 4, 7, 10, 13, 16, 19, 26, you are the histrionic type.

If you answered YES to at least five out of questions 2, 5, 8, 11, 14, 17, 20, 22, 24, you are egocentric.

If you answered YES to at least five out of questions 3, 6, 9, 12, 15, 18, 21, 23, 25, you are an 'orphan'.

The more YES answers you give in each of the above series, the more you fit that profile. Don't be surprised if you seem to fit more than one profile – that's quite normal. Just read the profile corresponding to your 'best' score (or the corresponding profiles if you score equally in more than one).

The histrionic
The term histrionic derives from the Latin *histrio*, meaning a comedian, boaster, or even a cheat. When you are deprived of love, you tend to become hysterical. You burst into tears for nothing, or you fly into a rage. For those around you, it's heaven or hell. You are either in the depths of despair, or you are on Cloud Nine. You always trust people too quickly and too soon. You will fall under the spell of anyone with a strong personality. You think that they can offer magic solutions to all your problems. And after it's all over, you feel totally let down. As a result, all your relationships are generally stormy and insincere.

What can you do about it? Your problem is first of all that you are over-emotional, you suffer from overwhelming feelings. You are obsessed with strong emotions and get carried away with them.

You are soon bored by routine (no challenge) and tenderness (no passion). At the drop of a hat, you will be out there in search of something new and stimulating. You make a drama out of every insignificant event. So how do you cure yourself?

Get a grip on your emotions. Good or bad, they are always excessive and this stops you from seeing people and events in a realistic light. You must learn moderation. To help you, there are a number of tricks you can use every time you feel your stress levels rising or you think you are about to behave foolishly. Try to relax and take a deep breath. Breathe out through your mouth and sit quietly to compose yourself. Close your eyes and detach yourself from everything around you for a few seconds. Then pinch yourself hard to force your mind away from whatever is preoccupying you. If you do this on a regular basis, you will, in a very short time, feel more relaxed and less vulnerable and you should react less dramatically to other people's behaviour.

Use your imagination (after all, you have quite a lot of it). Imagine you are an actress playing a role, perhaps a 'princess', or a 'victim'. (This should be easy for you – you're always feeling that you are either adored or abused and ignored.) Other people find you full of warmth but a little superficial. So try to show them that you regard life as a game, a show, in which you are just a good actress. By detaching yourself in this way, you should regain some credibility amongst them. The real you will certainly seem more sincere.

Play everything down. Keep your super sexy clothing for parties or the bedroom. It only creates a scene at the office or if you are out shopping. Also, stop being sexually provocative (another forte of yours) when it's not appropriate to the situation. You won't find love by behaving like a tease or an easy lay. Let your words get the message across instead of your body. Stop hugging every casual acquaintance as if he was the love of your life and don't be tempted to wrap yourself all round a man just because he's bought you lunch – even if it was delicious. Try to explain more what you feel and why. If you describe everything and everyone, including your latest man, as 'absolutely gorgeous', eventually it becomes meaningless. Think about what you really want to say and say only what you know is true.

The egocentric
When you are let down in love, you become terribly narcissistic. It does have its advantages (you end up looking particularly glamorous) but it can be quite inconvenient. You spend all your money on clothes, cosmetics and beauty treatments ... And yet, despite all the care you take of your body and the time you put into your appearance, you are never satisfied with what you see in the mirror. Deep down, you don't think you look good and you are scared that no one will find you attractive. No matter how much your friends or would-be partners try to reassure you, you simply cannot believe anyone could find you in the least seductive.

What can you do about it? When people are acutely narcissistic, the real problem is that they are being passive. They behave as if they were objects (sexual or otherwise), desirable goods, rather than people. That's why other people's opinions assume such importance. 'If they don't like me, they won't buy.' So what do you do about it?

Set yourself objectives and role-models that are realistic for you. Remember, it isn't necessary in life to accomplish great things or achieve perfection. Also remember that anyone truly exceptional has either got exceptional talent or has put in exceptional effort. You don't win first prize in an international music competition or get to be the first woman on the moon just by accident. So, do you want to make life a struggle? Not really? Well then, forget about anything that's obviously beyond your capabilities. Stop looking enviously at top models. You will never have such long legs, such perfect breasts, or their success, power, brilliance or beauty – but it's pretty overrated anyway. Try to put things into perspective – after all, it's quite possible that they may be absolutely miserable, despite being so beautiful.

Take compliments for what they are. Don't try to read things into them all the time. Don't imagine love or desire where there isn't any. If your boss congratulates you on a job well done, don't translate this as: 'He obviously fancies me something rotten but he's too shy to tell me.' If your butcher says 'There you go, love, I always keep a nice bit for you', don't think that this means he wants you to come up with a nice bit for him.

Stop trying to look at yourself from other people's point of view. You have always tended to centre everything on how people regard you. You turn everything back on to yourself: for example, if someone says 'I love you' or 'I want you', you start asking yourself: 'Why does he love me?', 'Why does he want me?' You must learn to change your perspective, move the focus away from yourself and ask yourself 'Do I love him?', 'Do I want him?' Instantly, that completely changes how you look at other people. Suddenly they exist in their own right and not only in relation to you. They are not there solely to give worth to you or to serve your objectives.

The orphan

You are so hungry for love, it makes you submissive, you become a real doormat. You give up your whole personality. You no longer have tastes, ideas, or preferences of your own. Clothes, work, home, holidays, you let other people decide on everything. Sometimes it works out quite well, especially if your partner likes the same things as you do. Fine if he's crazy about sailing and you adore anything to do with being out in the fresh air. Not so good, though, if he turns out to be mad about white-water rafting and your idea of heaven is an afternoon in a museum.

What can you do about it? Fear and an inability to deal with being alone are at the heart of your problem. You will do almost anything, sacrifice whatever it takes not to be abandoned or left behind. This goes not only for your way of life but also, and worse still, for your way of thinking. You may be surrounded by people, all giving you advice and opinions, but it only makes you feel more lost. You can't agree with all of them and you don't know how to be your own woman. You must learn to be alone. Here's how.

Stop volunteering for all the dirty work. Don't leap to your feet when someone asks who's going to do the washing up after a dinner for 12 or who is going to miss lunch to photocopy an urgent file. People don't love you any more for the fact that you take on all the chores. On the contrary, it devalues you in their eyes. Only in fairy tales are princes charming to Cinderellas. So bite your tongue before offering your services. If you think you're not going to be able to say no, hide. Or else, do what men do: do it so badly that everyone will immediately stop asking you.

Learn to manage your time for yourself. It's typical of people who are overdependent on others that they can never organise anything in advance because they are so afraid of either missing something better or upsetting someone by having to refuse a last-minute invitation. Just get on with the jobs you are supposed to be doing. If your time is precious, it's because you are too. Other people will not be offended if you can't always be at their disposal. In fact, by making yourself less accessible, you will increase your value to them. Force yourself to have your answering machine on – permanently (it will be difficult, but you must learn to do it). Then, instead of hanging around waiting for every call, you will have the choice of answering, or calling back when you – **you** – want to. This way, you'll be able to do what you really want to do instead of wasting time on people you don't really care about.

Train yourself to do things on your own (even if you are in a relationship). Start with something easy: the cinema (at last, you can go and see a film you like!) or music (you can, finally, keep that promise you made to yourself about learning to play the piano again). As you become more confident by yourself, it will be easier to get the hairdresser to cut your hair in the style you want, rather than the way he thinks it should be. In shops, sales assistants won't be able to talk you into buying something that you know is overpriced and too small for you. And your partner will suddenly find you more desirable because he knows you no longer need him.

ARE MEN SCARED OF YOU?

If you have a good EQ, you make those around you feel confident and comfortable. Do men feel good in your company or, on the contrary, are they worried about not making the grade – or even too scared to try? This test will help you to assess your capacity to attract men or make them want to run away. Add up your scores and see how scary you are.

SCORE:
Add up the number of As, Bs, and Cs you score, then look at the corresponding assessments on pages 100–102. If you have less than two points' difference between two scores, read both profiles – you have something of both in you.

You see a little Lagerfeld suit to die for. You:
- A Wait for the sales.
- B Drop hints: 'Well, if you don't know what to get me for my birthday ...'
- C Get out your credit card.

The last time you had an argument with your partner, you:
- A Moved into the spare room.
- B Threatened to leave him.
- C Threw something at him.

You think that, overall, his friends are:
- A Quite nice.
- B A bit of a nuisance.
- C Absolutely useless.

The worst thing you ever did to a man was to:
- A Make a scene in public.
- B Disappear for three days.
- C Hit him.

You've just had dinner together for the first time. The bill arrives, so you:
  A   Go and freshen up whilst he pays.
  B   Offer to go Dutch.
  C   Tell him: 'Next time it's on me.'

Your hair is:
  A   Long.
  B   Down to your shoulders.
  C   Quite short.

You find it hard to:
  A   Tell lies.
  B   Endure being humiliated.
  C   Control your anger.

As a child, you remember being punished:
  A   Rarely.
  B   More often by your mother.
  C   More often by your father.

He's sorry, he can't be with you for your birthday party. You tell him:
  A   'It doesn't matter, darling, we'll celebrate together when you come back.'
  B   'Anyway, with all the people who are coming we wouldn't be able to spend that much time together.'
  C   'That's such a shame, everyone will be there, even my ex ...'

To wind him up, you would be prepared to 'confess' that:
  A   In your teens, you had a sexual relationship with a girlfriend.
  B   You really like being tied up to make love.
  C   You have been to bed with two men at the same time.

He can't get an erection. You reassure him but you can't stop thinking:

  A 'It's awful, he doesn't love me.'
  B 'Poor love, he gets tired quickly ...'
  C 'He never was much good ...'

You know exactly how to:

  A Make him cry.
  B Make him laugh.
  C Make him angry.

When you feel lost, you need:

  A Someone to hold your hand.
  B To be alone.
  C Someone to lust after.

Your favourite position for making love is:

  A Him on top.
  B Lying on your side, your back to his front.
  C You on top.

The very first time you made love, it was:

  A To please someone.
  B Inevitable – it had to happen one day.
  C As a dare.

You can count your sexual partners:

  A On one hand.
  B On both your hands.
  C You need your toes as well.

In the last 12 months, you have made love with:

  A One person.
  B Two people.
  C Rather a lot of people.

You have most often:

  A Been the one who was dumped.
  B Chucked one man for another.
  C Been the one to break up.

You think it would be okay to:
  A Have a child with a man to please him.
  B Get pregnant without telling him.
  C Have a child without the father.

He doesn't have the means to take you on holiday in the spring, so you:
  A Stay at home: after all, the important thing is to be with him.
  B Go away for a week without him.
  C Accept an invitation from one of your exes.

When you live with a man, you usually:
  A Think you can trust him until he proves otherwise.
  B Think that he's sincere for now, but …
  C Assume he's never entirely honest with you.

Your mum drilled it into you that men:
  A Are all the same.
  B Must be controlled.
  C Cannot be relied on.

If he points out that your first boyfriend seems to still be in love with you, you say:
  A 'And yet we only exchanged a few kisses …'
  B 'He's never forgotten our nights together …'
  C 'I nearly married him …'

Clearly, you like each other a lot, but he hasn't dared touch you yet, so:
  A You take him by the hand.
  B You kiss him on the lips.
  C You slip into his bed.

Your lover is astonished at how easily you manage to get into a rather unusual sexual position. You tell him:
  A 'I learn fast with you …'
  B 'I have always been very supple …'
  C 'My ex and I used to do this all the time …'

He surprises you with a weekend in Venice. You tell him:
- A   'I always wanted to go there, but I was waiting for someone like you.'
- B   'I am so happy to be going back, I have wonderful memories from there.'
- C   'I hope you booked us into the Danieli, I've been to four or five hotels in Venice, and that's the one I really prefer.'

You slip up by calling him by your ex's name. You say:
- A   'I wasn't thinking about that David, I was thinking about David from the office.'
- B   'You know me, I always get names mixed up ...'
- C   'It's probably because I am having dinner with him tonight.'

He invites you for a Valentine's Day meal to his favourite Italian restaurant. You say:
- A   'I have heard about it, apparently it's really good.'
- B   'Are you absolutely sure it's the best? I've always been told Machino's is better.'
- C   'The best is Machino's, but you can only reserve if they know you.'

Highest total As

Men are rarely scared of you. In fact, you fit the traditional image of a man's dream woman: sweet, reserved and understanding. They find you most reassuring. But does this come naturally to you? Is it the result of the old-fashioned way you were brought up? Or is it a seduction strategy? Either way, it doesn't matter. They think you're sweet and fragile and that's what matters.

You know how to make men feel good. You flatter their ego to get what you want or submit happily when it suits you. You use all the old tricks and feminine wiles and it works. When he's with you, a man feels totally confident of his virility. He can open his big protective wings, pretend he's a knight in shining armour and he knows he's not going to have it all thrown in his face. You are quite happy to let him empty the bin, carry your suitcases, open the bottle of wine or take sole responsibility for the bills. You are prepared to overlook his (many) faults and his bachelor habits as long as he plays the man's role.

So, it's hardly a surprise that he's not scared. Living with you is a joy. You are patient, tolerant and peace-loving. But perhaps, just sometimes, you are too indulgent. It does a man no harm to be scared occasionally. Otherwise, he thinks anything goes. So give a little tug on the ball and chain now and then to make sure he knows it's there. He'll become less inclined to overstep the mark.

Highest total Bs
Men are a little scared of you. Just enough to make them respect you. They look at you, they listen to you and see that you have lived life, you have your own ways and needs. They sense that there's an iron fist in that velvet glove. They realise they can't just do as they want.

You are nice but you are no mug. You may be in love but that doesn't mean you will accept everything his way. Your attitude makes macho men very insecure but the rest appreciate it. Getting on with a woman who has personality and character is much more worthwhile than living with a docile little girl who makes life too easy. Of course, sometimes you can be so sharp with him, he doesn't know what to do: he's scared of setting you off and he dreads losing you. Good! It will stop him from thinking he can treat you as a mere chattel and he will certainly hesitate before pushing his luck with you. On the contrary, he'll make more of an effort because he cares about you. He still wants you like crazy after the fateful 317 days and 16 hours that, statistically, marks the average length of a passionate relationship. And, ten years on, he'll be as attentive as he was in the beginning. So, don't be afraid of scaring him every now and then. Even if you don't do it on purpose.

Highest total Cs
Men are really scared of you. Even though they may not actually run away, they never feel really confident. There is always something

about you that is too much for them to cope with. Too beautiful, too intelligent, too independent. Or, too aggressive, too unpredictable ...

A man is never sure how you are going to react, never assured of where he stands with you. He often has the impression of being superfluous, he thinks: 'She doesn't need me.' He's scared of not coming up to your standards (in bed or anywhere else), of causing a rift without meaning to. He's permanently on the edge of his seat, thinking 'If this doesn't work, she's going to leave me.'

Actually, you scare him a lot without even meaning to. Perhaps it's because you've been making your own decisions for so long, you've forgotten how to make concessions to other people. Perhaps it's because you are not particularly trusting, you've had enough of being taken for a ride. So you appear inaccessible. The trouble is, it means you always have problems keeping a man. Your relationship quickly turns into a competition, a power struggle. It's useless for you to try to pretend to be a lamb: you are just not credible as a sweet little girl. However, you can get rid of a lot of his anxiety by gently explaining to him how you like to function as part of a couple. A man is always less scared when he knows what to expect ...

ARE YOU CONTENT TO BE A WOMAN?

You have a good EQ when you have an appropriate awareness of yourself and your relationships with the opposite sex. According to Freud, each little girl thinks that because she doesn't have a penis, she's lacking something. Hopefully, we've gone beyond that way of thinking; what certainly is important is that a girl should grow up believing that she has something of her own that is worth just as much. Otherwise, later on, her behaviour as a woman and her relationships with men may be adversely affected. So, have you come to terms with yourself? Let's see ...

Once again, read the statements and tick the response that most applies to you.

SCORE:
Add up the number of As, Bs, Cs and Ds you score, then look at the corresponding assessments on pages 107–10.

On the beach, you hate the number of:
A   Fat topless women.
B   Little girls wearing bras.
C   Men with lots of thick, black body hair.
D   Little boys not wearing trunks.

Your most erogenous zone is:
A   Your breasts.
B   Your bum.
C   Your genitals.
D   Your mouth.

Your recurring fantasy involves:
- A Making love in public.
- B Being on the game.
- C Raping a woman.
- D Forcing yourself on a man.

If you were a pervert, you would be:
- A An exhibitionist.
- B A slave.
- C A woman with a whip.
- D An eternal virgin.

You often have the same erotic dream about:
- A Famous people.
- B Another woman.
- C Sex organs without a face.
- D The man who shares your bed.

You have problems accepting another person's:
- A Inferiority complex.
- B Aggressiveness.
- C Guilty feelings.
- D Self-satisfaction.

You think it would be okay to:
- A Bring up a child without a father.
- B Adopt a child.
- C Have children from different fathers.
- D Not have any children.

The man in your life has faults that:
- A You are going change.
- B Will never change.
- C With time, will sort themselves out.
- D Can be improved, with your help.

You feel worst when you:
- A Lose your temper.
- B Burst into tears.
- C Feel dreadfully ashamed of something.
- D Are disgusted by something.

You are most worn down by:
- A Routine.
- B Tantrums.
- C Competition.
- D Questions.

When you were a child:
- A Both your parents used to smack you.
- B Your mother used to smack you more often.
- C Your father sometimes used to smack you.
- D You were never smacked.

You cannot stand a man who:
- A Is indifferent to your charms.
- B Criticises you.
- C Is married.
- D Is not up to it.

The sense that gives you most pleasure is:
- A Sight.
- B Touch.
- C Smell.
- D Taste.

The deadly sin that most characterises you is:
- A Gluttony.
- B Anger.
- C Lust.
- D Envy.

To build a life together, you need to have:
- A   Knowledge.
- B   Ability.
- C   Commitment.
- D   Will.

If you feel intimidated, you tend to:
- A   Burst into tears.
- B   Become aggressive.
- C   Go bright red.
- D   Talk non-stop.

Your worst nightmare is when you dream that:
- A   You fall into space.
- B   You are naked in the middle of a crowd.
- C   You are being followed by something/someone.
- D   You lose all your teeth.

You were brought up:
- A   As an only child.
- B   With brothers and sisters.
- C   With one or more sisters.
- D   With one or more brothers.

You are most concerned about:
- A   Being admired for your physical appearance.
- B   Your success and your personal reputation.
- C   Being abandoned.
- D   Your sexual partner's fidelity.

You particularly hate:
- A   Not getting what you want.
- B   Being kept waiting.
- C   Disagreeing with others.
- D   Someone making decisions for you.

If a colleague in the office touched your bum, you would:
A   Follow him back to his place.
B   Kick him where it hurts.
C   Have to admit you had been leading him on.
D   Report him for assault.

It's exciting when a man:
A   Has come-to-bed eyes.
B   Looks threatening.
C   Swears.
D   Appears indifferent to you.

You have to admit you once:
A   Went shoplifting.
B   Drove while you were drunk.
C   Slept with a stranger.
D   Physically threatened someone.

When it comes to love-making you think:
A   Sex is boring.
B   You have nothing more to learn about sex.
C   All men are idiots.
D   You have it all to learn.

Highest total As
You are somewhat narcissistic and you have a subconscious desire for power. Your desire for control is projected on to others. Strong men are your preference, men with power, men of the moment. You enjoy making them submit to your whims, and they usually fulfil your desires. You are full of your own importance, you tend to overestimate your abilities and exaggerate your achievements, thinking that everything about you is exceptional, even your problems.

You can adapt your outlook and your behaviour to suit any situation. You intuitively know how to get on to the same wavelength as other people, you can always find the right words and the right attitude to inspire sympathy and make people like you. You will use every trick in the book to seduce someone and you frequently resort to using your charms to get what you want.

You are often quite vain and very anxious for compliments: you look for reassurance in other people's eyes. You tend to worry about your reputation, yearn for success and long for approval and outright praise from those around you. Sensitivity to criticism is another factor in your make-up, but most of the time you conceal your anger or shame behind an exterior of calm indifference.

Appearances are important to you and you take an excessive amount of time over the care of your body and your clothes. You do not enjoy being alone and often find it difficult to plan or do things on your own. An addiction to love means you have a need to share and feel loved and protected.

Highest total Bs
You are macho, very dominant and masculine in your behaviour and outlook. A woman who loves power, you have a need to take your revenge on men, to beat them at their own game. You are self-assured, resolute, rash and ready for any challenge. You love to get involved in competition, both on the sportsfield and professionally. You tend to drive fast, both in your car and your life.

You have envied men since you were a little girl (they could wee further). As a teenager, you were a tomboy or one of the lads. Even today, you can proudly claim that your best friends are male. That allows you to avoid sexual confrontations with a clear conscience. You have always been a little ashamed of your body, your femininity. Sexually, you don't want 'to be had', as you put it. As a result, when you are aroused, you fulfil your fantasies and your desires in a rather macho style: 'I take what I want, then I throw it away.'

You avoid falling in love because feelings are too complicated for you and you know that you can end up badly hurt. Instead you are inclined to be attracted to impossible loves and men you know you can never have: men you meet on aeroplanes, very-much-married family men, men with oversized muscles and a pea-sized brain, men not fit to be seen, let alone taken out, men who are simply not presentable in public. You can keep trying to idealise them, imagine they are princes disguised as frogs, but it's no use. In the end, you are always disappointed. And so you continue, between long periods of celibacy, to look for a man, a real one, the one who would be at least your equal. Don't give up, however, he's out there somewhere. But you may find him more easily if you try looking for strength of character rather than powerful physique in your man.

Highest total Cs

You are over-sexed, yet you feel that you have no great value. You compensate by going overboard with anything ultra-feminine. You are a real macho man's dream, a pre-feminism survivor reincarnated in the shape of a submissive woman.

Attractive and seductive, you tend to give in to every male fantasy and desire. You can play any role: princess or pervert, virgin or whore. Because you are so anxious for compliments and praise, you may be prepared to be almost too obliging. With your great need to be admired, you sometimes overdo your super-sexy look, your sexual provocation. You try (with success) to make men mad for you, especially those with the strongest personalities, the most virile ones. But, as soon as they fall for you, you cease to have any regard for them.

You are forever looking for new experiences; your affairs develop quickly but the routine of a relationship soon bores you. Impressionable and easily influenced, you frequently escape into romantic fantasies.

You do not seem to make a connection between sex and tenderness. You are not able to love what you desire, nor desire what you love. You have no hang-ups or sexual inhibitions, and are even something of an exhibitionist. In fact, the less you are emotionally involved, the more pleasure you get out of sex. But physical satisfaction is not the key to contentment. You may need to look for something deeper in your relationships if you are to end your restless search for gratification.

Highest total Ds

You satisfy your desire for superiority by castrating men – figuratively at least. Self-sufficient and rather egocentric, you don't like to let anyone decide for you and you have an often excessive way of showing that you are mentally and emotionally independent: you don't need anyone in your life.

Ambitious and super-efficient, you react very strongly to criticism, even when it's justified, and you are very quick and forthright in your counter-attacks. You may not have much of a sense of humour. You find it difficult to relax; you are always on your guard. Other people, especially men, are seen as rivals and enemies. You enjoy using men for sex and, if you are gay, you enjoy taking their women. You are serious-minded and coolly rational and there is rarely much affection or tenderness in your relationships. You are too scared of losing your independence and your control of events.

You generally avoid any kind of intimacy, except in a rare instance of absolute trust. As far as you're concerned, love and emotion bring nothing but problems. Your needs, mainly characterised by an almost tyrannical desire to be loved, have something scary about them. They make most men run (certainly the strong ones), but they do attract some, particularly masochists. However, nothing and no one seems able to satisfy you completely.

Your affairs tend to be based on domination and submission and even sado-masochism, and war frequently breaks out between you and your partner. Reconciliations are passionate but brief: you spend more time tearing each other apart and breaking up. Even when you are in a good mood, you can't help hurting your loved one's pride or dampening his (or her) good spirits. You are frequently oversensitive, deeply suspicious, you feel easily despised and you often display an almost pathological jealousy. If your score is very high, you may be the sort who bears grudges, who refuses any kind of compromise and cuts short any attempt at reconciliation. Beware of letting your anger and desire for revenge get the better of your self-control. You will need to calm down and trust people more if you are to build any lasting intimate relationships.

DO YOU HAVE A GRUDGE AGAINST MEN?

A good EQ means being able to read other people's feelings, but also your own. All women have, at some time or another, had a good reason to hold something against men. Some women will readily admit to having a complete down on men and feel that they can no longer trust them at all. And yet the majority say they do not bear any lasting grudge or feelings of resentment towards men. They say they still love them. But do they really – or have they got bad feelings about one man in particular, or this or that type? What about you? Could it be that you have a grudge against men without knowing or wanting it?

Read each of the following statements and decide to what degree it applies to you. Take note of the letter in the column you choose in each case and keep score.

SCORE:
Add up your totals of As, Bs, Cs and Ds, then look at the profile corresponding to your largest total on pages 114–19. If you have less than three points' difference between two totals, read both profiles – you have characteristics of both.

	Definitely not	Not really	Some-what	Totally
You think men are mainly attracted by your figure.	A	C	B	D
You are horrified that your partner uses your toothbrush.	D	C	B	A

	Definitely not	Not really	Some-what	Totally
You don't hesitate to use your charms (even bare them a little) to advance your career.	A	C	B	D
You often doubt your friends' loyalty.	D	B	C	A
When you are in love, you tend to put your loved one on a pedestal.	A	B	C	D
You are always afraid that your secrets might be used against you.	D	C	B	A
You find it difficult to accept that your partner likes to have an occasional evening out alone with a friend (male or female).	A	D	B	C
You burst into tears over the slightest emotional upset.	A	B	C	D
You believe that guys are given a better deal by society in general.	D	C	B	A
You enjoy sexual provocation, especially at inappropriate times and places.	D	C	A	B
As a child, you were a bit of a tomboy.	D	C	B	A

	Definitely not	Not really	Some-what	Totally
You think that when you love someone, you have the right to ask for anything.	A	B	D	C
To hold on to your man, you are prepared to turn a blind eye to his infidelities.	A	B	C	D
You often have problems with other women.	D	B	C	A
You always speak your mind.	D	C	B	A
As a teenager, you and your father were often partners in crime.	D	B	C	A
You have a weakness for sexy clothes.	A	C	D	B
It would bother you to be financially dependent on a man.	D	C	B	A
You think it's quite possible to make love to someone you don't love.	D	C	B	A
You often turn and look when an attractive man passes you.	D	A	C	B
It's embarrassing to see a man cry.	B	C	D	A

	Definitely not	Not really	Some-what	Totally
You would rather your partner was unfaithful to you with a man than with a woman.	D	C	B	A
In your fantasies, you are often the only woman with a group of men on an island or a boat.	A	C	B	D
Your first sexual experience was a catastrophe.	B	D	C	A
You like to pay the bill when you go to a restaurant with your partner.	D	B	C	A

Highest total As

You are the iron lady: deep down, consciously or not, you see all men as rivals or enemies. You hold a grudge against them, you have some kind of revenge to take on them. You don't trust men and you don't expect anything good to come from them, other than the occasional sexual satisfaction. You expect them to conform willy-nilly to your desires from the first date until you finally fall into bed and consummate the relationship. It's no use them even trying to run the show.

You may or may not admit it to yourself, but you often think that sex can be humiliating for at least one of the people involved and you'd rather humiliate the man before he humiliates you. Sometimes you do this by turning men on, only to go cruelly cold on them as soon as they think that they're in with a chance. At other times, you may do it by making fun of their manhood.

Generally, you like your men to be a little effeminate. You avoid real men. You are too afraid of the backlash.

Mistress of your relationships, you are even more in control in your daily affairs. You don't feel that you have to be part of a couple to be a success in life. You can see yourself being quite happy living alone (even if you have a child). You would regard having to struggle in life as a stimulus, not an obstacle.

At work, you tend to be too competitive, too systematically aggressive towards the men. And it's not simply to defend a stance or obtain an advantage – that would be understandable and perfectly acceptable. But it seems that you are trying to show them that you are stronger than they are – and you are doing that to hurt them.

Your problem: you cannot accept that men generally get a better deal. As far as you're concerned they've been in a dominant position in society for too long and you find that totally unfair (and you are right). You are deeply angered by this and try to protest by demonstrating manly characteristics of your own.

The solution: you want power – so take it. But don't simply try to behave like a man. It has been said that 'Forgiveness is more virile than punishment.' So learn to forgive. If you must fight, don't do it with the men in your life. Don't try to take revenge on your partner for the humiliations and wrongs you've received from other people. Fight for good causes. There are plenty of them around – try starting with battered women (and children), sexual harassment, equal pay and pensions for women … That should help you to work off your frustrations.

Highest total Bs
You don't trust men. And yet you only occasionally admit it to yourself. The rest of the time you say you love them. What you really mean is that you can't do without them, at least not socially.

On the whole, you can manage quite well. You don't need anyone to bring home the bacon, fill in your tax forms or put up shelves for you – you are very independent and prefer to be self-sufficient. On the other hand, you do have physical needs and going without a man for too long depresses you. One month of enforced celibacy feels like a life sentence. So, you do like to enjoy a good sex life, but always on your terms. The man in your life – and in your bed – must learn to keep a low profile, give in to your demands. You may turn nasty if he makes the slightest attempt to question you.

If someone doesn't agree with you, you immediately think it's because they are trying to be mean to you. Then you tend to go into oversensitive mode and refuse to recognise any overtures of friendship and rebuff any attempts at reconciliation. You rarely show any understanding, tolerance or patience, that wouldn't be your style. You prefer to dish out threats (subtle as they may sometimes be) and ultimatums. 'Take it or leave it,' you yell, 'There's always plenty more fish in the sea.'

Your problem: since you insist on reigning by terror, the only men you attract are real weeds. You think you are loved and respected but, in reality, they are just plain scared of you. When you come across your real soulmate, the one you've been waiting for, you let him get away. What's worse, your explosive aggressiveness probably made him run away. You may look like an angel, but men know they're really holding an unexploded bomb.

The solution: you have to understand that your aggressive attitude is a defensive reflex. You just don't have enough confidence in your own femininity. Deep down you are fragile, vulnerable, scared of being hurt, rejected (you may very well have had a particularly hard and demanding father). You do have flings and affairs but you often end up sabotaging your own relationship by ending it yourself because you are afraid of getting involved.

Also, you tend to overreact all the time – the slightest false move by your partner and you go off like an atomic bomb. You must learn to control yourself. If you really can't hold in your anger and frustration, go and explode somewhere else. Avoid arguing yourself into a corner. You must understand that in every relationship, power struggles are inevitable. You would find everything a lot easier to manage if you could just get it into your head that if a man really loves you, he also loves you for your faults. And if he doesn't, he's not worth it.

Highest total Cs

You are highly demanding: you want the best out of every man you love. Sensible, intelligent, funny, responsible, serious, handsome ... the picture you paint of your requirements is enough to make strong men pale with fright. Your friends tell you you'll never find all those qualities in one man. But that's because they haven't reckoned with the Pygmalion in you. You feel confident that you can take any man (with some basic good points, of course) and shape him into your ideal. For obvious reasons, you tend to attract rather childish guys, the ones that are still developing, not to say underdeveloped – other kinds of men can't take too much of you, certainly not for long.

Unfortunately, when you do get a man you tend to ask too much. You are always moving the goal posts, raising the stakes. No matter what he does, how hard he tries, he can never be quite up to it. And since he can't satisfy you, he obviously gets fed up. You constantly criticise him, accuse him of not trying, and if he doesn't manage to put you on Cloud Nine in bed every night or his salary in the upper tax bracket, you accuse him of not loving you. He has to put up with your constant moods of disappointment, suspicion and jealousy, so in the long run it's hardly surprising that he gives up on you.

Your problem: deep down, you don't have much respect for men (usually the result of having had a weak father and a dominant mother). You are convinced that they need to be controlled and treated like some sort of lower life-form. After all, you say, it's for their own good: a man is nothing without a woman like you behind him.

The solution: turn the problem around. If a guy satisfied all your demands, gave in to all your whims, you wouldn't want him any more. You would be the first to accuse him of not being a real man.

In fact, your idea of a real man is a contradiction in terms. You want him to be both malleable and strong, obedient and resistant. So stop asking a man for more than he can give and, most of all, don't expect him to be perfect. Accept the fact that he has his limits, that he can probably just manage to be a passably sweet angel – but only sometimes – and a bit of a sexual beast – but only occasionally. Like you, men have their faults and you have to accept that when you choose them. After all, when you buy a pair of shoes, you don't buy them one size too small, thinking they will stretch to fit your feet. So take notice of any alarm bells that ring when you meet. Stop telling yourself: 'He'll be different with me ...' Accept that you can't really change a man – at the most, you may just manage to modify him slightly.

Highest total Ds
You simply adore men. They are so delicious, so extraordinary, so cute. You are prepared to forgive them anything. Women don't come more understanding, more devoted and more tolerant than you. You never want to upset them or create problems for them. You agree with everything, even – or perhaps I should say especially – when you think they are wrong.

When you love a man, you display the patience of an angel. You hang on his every word. You applaud every move he makes. You turn a blind eyes to all his sins, however great they may be. At the slightest critical observation ('Wasn't the roast slightly overcooked, dear?') you reach instantly for the hair shirt and throw yourself at his feet to be reprimanded. To start with, men love it. It boosts their ego and flatters their virility. How can they resist such adoration? But in the long run your constant self-criticism (you just never get things right), apologising (you are sorry you're not up to it), and tears (you don't want to lose him) end up making **him** feel guilty ('She doesn't deserve to be made to feel like this, I am such a bastard to her'). Finally, you turn what was a fairly normal guy into some kind of selfish monster who's not feeling terribly good about himself. By running yourself down, you run him down too.

Your problem: deep down, you see yourself as a victim (even if you often play the role of a princess). You have a negative view of women and of your own femininity (probably you had a weak mother). You tend to have it in for men because you think (subconsciously) that they despise you. Convinced that they cannot really love you, you try to make them feel sorry for you.

The solution: you must rebuild a positive image of yourself. To do that, you must throw yourself into any activities that you enjoy and that make you feel good. You must learn to feel that you don't owe anything to anybody. You must learn to do things for yourself instead of constantly trying to seduce or please a man.

You obviously have some talents, so concentrate on developing them – aim for success. Be a bit more demanding, too. Don't stand for any behaviour or remarks from him that put you down. You may think you can handle it, but you are kidding yourself. In the long run, resentment and poor self-esteem build up and you find you lose the respect of other people too. Contrary to what you may imagine, they respect you now a lot more than you think.

WHAT DO YOU NEED TO BE HAPPY?

It is a known fact that having a good EQ can make you happier. Sometimes you feel you have everything that should make you happy, but at other times it seems that you are really just stuck in a routine, not too sure of yourself and desperately needing someone to love you. To be truly happy, you have to understand what is missing in your life – and everyone's needs are different. This section will help you to discover what you need to make **you** happy.

Choose the answer that most closely resembles your likely response and keep score.

SCORE:
Add up the number of As, Bs, Cs and Ds you score, then read the profile corresponding to your highest total on pages 125–8. If you have only two or three points' difference between two totals, read both profiles as you have characteristics of both.

Real love:
  A Is what you're feeling right now.
  B Happens once in a lifetime.
  C Doesn't exist.
  D Is too complicated.

If a genie offered to grant you a wish, you would ask:
  A To have enough money to stop working.
  B To meet Prince Charming.
  C To be immortal.
  D To be ten years younger.

When you are dreadfully nervous:
    A Your skin breaks out.
    B You have difficulty in breathing.
    C Your stomach plays up.
    D You suffer muscular spasms.

You rarely have time to:
    A Get bored.
    B Catch up.
    C Relax.
    D Waste.

You don't have much confidence in:
    A Politicians.
    B Judges.
    C Priests.
    D Journalists.

You would quite like to get to know:
    A An extraterrestrial.
    B Jesus Christ.
    C A friendly genie.
    D A good plumber.

You are most scared at the thought of:
    A Being ill.
    B Being lonely.
    C Dying.
    D Getting old.

The thing that makes you most unhappy is:
    A Intolerance.
    B Selfishness.
    C Poverty.
    D Insecurity.

You are most worried when you think about:
- A Extreme right-wing politicians.
- B Contaminated blood.
- C Chernobyl.
- D Mad cow disease.

When you are under stress, you tend to suffer from:
- A Mood swings.
- B Anxiety.
- C Migraines.
- D Insomnia.

Your most frequent nightmare involves you:
- A Being rooted to the spot, unable to move.
- B Being chased by someone who is trying to kill you.
- C Finding yourself naked in front of everyone.
- D Losing all your teeth.

Your favourite pet would be:
- A A cat.
- B A dog.
- C A bird.
- D A fish.

You were brought up by:
- A Both your parents.
- B Your father mainly.
- C Your mother alone.
- D Your grandparents.

You are more likely to buy a product if:
- A It is top quality.
- B The manufacturer financially supports a humanitarian cause.
- C It's a brand you like.
- D It comes with eco-biological guarantees.

You would like to have more spare time to:

    A   Do the gardening.
    B   Listen to music.
    C   Cook.
    D   Watch TV.

Your collection of books consists mainly of:

    A   Foreign literature.
    B   Romantic novels.
    C   Practical guides.
    D   Popular paperbacks.

Last weekend, you:

    A   Went to an exhibition.
    B   Had lunch at your mum's.
    C   Went shopping with a friend.
    D   Didn't go anywhere.

In your life at the moment, you have:

    A   One wonderful man.
    B   No one.
    C   Several men.
    D   A married man.

Your lover of three days invites you out at one hour's notice, but you are already doing something, so you:

    A   Suggest meeting tomorrow.
    B   Cancel everything to meet him.
    C   Take him with you.
    D   Meet up later.

In your opinion, your mother is:

    A   A real tonic.
    B   A bit of a limpet.
    C   Temperamental.
    D   A perfectionist.

Not a day goes by without you:
- A Being approached by a stranger in the street.
- B Thinking about your ex.
- C Asking yourself 'What's the use?'
- D Wondering about your future.

If you were going to spend 15 days in a Russian space ship, you would take:
- A Your make-up bag.
- B Your old teddy bear.
- C Some chocolate.
- D A lucky charm.

Happiness is:
- A An attitude of mind.
- B A question of luck.
- C Linked to success.
- D Not having anything to be unhappy about.

Even for the love of a man, you are not prepared to:
- A Give up your financial independence.
- B Break with your parents.
- C Give up your friends.
- D Drop everything to start a new life abroad.

The quickest way of breaking someone psychologically is to stop them from:
- A Sleeping.
- B Eating.
- C Speaking.
- D Seeing light.

The main reason you chose your job was:
- A Because you liked it.
- B To please your parents.
- C It was a complete accident.
- D Because it offered you security.

If you had a magic wand, you would change:
- A Your body.
- B Your parents.
- C Your sex.
- D Your whole life.

Highest total As

There's nothing missing in your life. Of course, it could be improved. If you had been born on a plane above the Atlantic, you would have been given free world travel for the rest of your life. A few pounds less, a few inches more in the right places, and you could have been a top model. Your partner could come home earlier, surprise you more often with a visit to a restaurant instead of saying: 'What's for dinner tonight?' Your boss could find it easier to praise you and give you a rise. You could win a fortune on the Lottery and lead a life of leisure on a Caribbean island. Yes, life would be much more pleasant without the troubles in Northern Ireland or Yugoslavia. But hell, we don't think about that every day. So if you do feel unhappy, it's because there's something not quite right in your head.

Just look at yourself objectively, you have every reason to be happy and, most of all, the ability to bounce back if things ever do go wrong. You have the happiness gene and an innate optimism that seem to function even when you get out on the wrong side of the bed. You are good at reasoning with yourself, keeping calm and staying positive in the face of an ordeal. So just try to stop and think every time you have an attack of the blues, when you are moaning about your lot or when you are tempted to go and see if the grass is greener on the other side. Life is pretty good to you, on the whole, so appreciate it!

Highest total Bs

You're lacking in the love department. Perhaps you have a lot of emotional baggage: absent, or simply indifferent, parents, a lonely childhood, a shortage of cuddles. Perhaps you have experienced a failed love affair, and have often been let down. As a result, you now feel awkward in your relationships with others, especially in your love life.

You are never sure that you are being really loved or will be loved ever again. You live alone but you don't handle it very well. Or perhaps you are in a relationship that is far from being idyllic. Your problem is that you are in a vicious circle: the more love you need, the more you ask and the more you ask, the more you scare people away. Your affairs and friendships often fizzle out. You find a perfect partner, you move in together but somehow it doesn't work out too well: you are so afraid of being abandoned, the relationship is full of tension, which only makes you more frustrated and insecure.

The only way to reverse this trend and get out of this cycle is for you to try to be less demanding. Your great need for love is always going to be part of you, there's nothing you can do about that. But you can learn to control it. First of all, you have to realise that your need is so great, no man is ever going to be able to love you enough – not in your eyes, anyway. So you must put things in perspective. Don't expect everything of him. You can also fulfil your emotional needs in other ways – through your family, your friends, even through making some kind of contribution to a humanitarian organisation or a charity. Learn to give instead of always wanting to receive. Learn to love without expecting anything in return – you will probably be pleasantly surprised at how good it feels.

Highest total Cs

Your life lacks direction. As a result, you're never sure of anything. You're not sure if you're making the right choice, doing the right thing, or even if you're going the right way. You find it difficult to make decisions and then stick to them, and you don't like getting really involved.

At work or in love, you always have some qualms, some doubts. You are constantly wondering what it's all for. Is life worth all the hassle? Should you be living in town when you could feel better settling in the country? Should you go on working for someone or would you be better working for yourself? Are you doing the right thing staying with your present man or would that lovely bloke from sales make you happier? As a result, you tend to grope your way through life, tinkering with each little thing as it comes along.

You don't seem to have a life plan, or even a definite code of conduct. You function in terms of the opportunities and occasions that present themselves. Obviously, you don't have faith in what you do, because you have no values or motivation. You are the sort of person who is always asking 'What's the good of it all?' You can make yourself unhappy over nothing.

What you need is some direction in life, something that would give it some substance. Set yourself some objectives: start looking for a job that is more than just a way of earning a living; think about having a baby; find something to interest you that is a real passion. You don't have to embrace religion or join a sect (although that might help). But start searching for something that will put some meaning into your life.

Highest total Ds
Your life needs change and variety. You are stuck in a rut in your daily routine: the same friends, the same faces, the same activities: you function in a closed circuit. You have probably kissed goodbye to your childhood dreams and your early ambitions. There are enough good things in your personal and professional life and you are content just to keep it that way, so you put effort into not making waves. That's all well and good: by remaining in your little world, you feel more secure. You automatically eliminate the possibilities of failure, the risk of getting hurt. You rarely have nasty surprises, but neither do you have great joys. You pass by a lot of good things because of your lack of curiosity, or possibly, in fact, because of your over-cautiousness. So you often miss the chance to change. You don't seize the opportunities to do better, to improve your situation.

So, in the end, you will get bored with your job and all the passion will go out of your relationships. You will probably also find that you are affected more badly than most by today's atmosphere of economic gloom. It is because you are so passive – you are so anxious about the things going on around you but you don't feel able to do anything to change them. You have to recognise that being happy isn't simply avoiding unhappiness. Some of it is down to you. So, 'Just do it!' as the advert says. Expand your horizons. Try something new. It doesn't matter if you do something stupid or make mistakes. You are a big girl now and if you fall, you should be able to land on your feet – or pick yourself up and start again.

PART 3

SPECIALLY FOR YOUR MAN

DO WOMEN REALLY LOVE YOU?

A good EQ makes for more real, deeper love relationships. Women often accuse men of lacking emotion and sensitivity when it comes to love. They tend to prefer men who are capable of showing their emotions, or expressing their feelings. Are you that type of man? Or, on the contrary, are you one of those who, whilst attractive, aren't necessarily charming? This test will help you to discover whether you are the sort of man women really love.

Read the following statements and tick your most likely response to each one.

SCORE:
Add up the number of As, Bs, Cs and Ds you score and read the profile that corresponds to the letter with the highest total on pages 134–8. If you have less than two points' difference between two letters, you have characteristics of both and should read both profiles.

Women accuse you of:

A   Always trying to get out of things.
B   Taking three hours to tell a story.
C   Not being generous enough with your compliments.
D   Always saying: 'I told you so!'

You would be most attracted to a woman by her:

A   Sheer enthusiasm.
B   Figure.
C   Eyes.
D   Voice.

Your mum is most likely to:

A   Always take your side.
B   Try to impose her tastes and ideas on you.
C   Arrive unannounced.
D   Call you day and night.

You think women are naturally:

A   Patient.
B   Brave.
C   Faithful.
D   Tolerant.

A woman would be most likely to forgive you for:

A   Forgetting her birthday.
B   Not bringing her breakfast in bed.
C   Using her toothbrush.
D   Constantly changing the TV channel with the remote.

When you cook for her, you most often make:

A   A mixed salad.
B   Spaghetti bolognese.
C   Burgers and chips.
D   A nut roast.

You think it's normal for a woman to:
- A   Be brilliant at maths.
- B   Believe in miracles.
- C   Earn less than a man.
- D   Share the bill at a restaurant.

You are her ideal partner because:
- A   You are good at DIY.
- B   You tell her you love her every day.
- C   You think she's beautiful.
- D   You do the washing up.

Women are particularly attracted by:
- A   Your intelligence.
- B   Your sense of humour.
- C   Your sense of responsibility.
- D   Your hunky good looks.

Women are most turned off by:
- A   Greasy hair.
- B   Unshaven stubble.
- C   Dandruff.
- D   The full-on approach.

You are most likely to accuse a woman of being too:
- A   Worried about her work.
- B   Nosey.
- C   Possessive.
- D   Unpredictable.

Physically, you would describe yourself as:
- A   Rather thin.
- B   Well-built.
- C   Muscular but not overdeveloped.
- D   Chubby.

Your hair is:
- A Black.
- B Brown.
- C Blond.
- D Red.

The thing about your appearance that women really love is:
- A Your eyes.
- B Your hairy body.
- C Your boxer shorts.
- D Your glasses.

Your usual dress style is:
- A Suit and tie.
- B Jeans.
- C Outrageous.
- D Casual sports clothes.

When you are with a woman you would not:
- A Swear.
- B Interrupt her.
- C Forget to hold the door open for her.
- D Fail to say 'Thank you' or 'Good morning'.

To indulge a woman's fantasy, you would be prepared to:
- A Let her make love with another man.
- B Take her by force.
- C Become her sexual slave.
- D Make love to her in front of other people.

Right now, you are:
- A Very much loved by one woman.
- B Pretty much in love yourself.
- C Seeing someone, but not on a regular basis.
- D Not attached.

You think it's really important to women that you:
    A Let them go out at night by themselves.
    B Appreciate their cooking.
    C Are faithful to them.
    D Tell them they are beautiful.

You are most likely to let a woman down by:
    A Being less attentive than in the beginning.
    B Not showing the same desire for her.
    C Failing to keep your promises.
    D Letting your appearance go.

In most cases, you have:
    A Left one woman for another.
    B Been involved with several women at the same time.
    C Been dumped.
    D Not managed to get as far as the bed.

The thing that has most changed women's lives in the last 20 years is:
    A Contraception.
    B Advances in household technology.
    C Cohabitation.
    D The simplification of divorce.

Women think it will bring them luck if they:
    A Find a four-leaf clover.
    B Break a mirror.
    C Touch a hunchback's hump.
    D Dab champagne behind their ears.

Women would like you better if you were:
    A A rocket scientist.
    B The owner of a big company.
    C A TV or film star.
    D A sports champion or a male model.

Women are most turned on by:
- A Your behaviour.
- B The way you talk.
- C Your physique.
- D The way you look at them.

Highest total As

Women really do love you. But you are so used to it that sometimes you don't even realise it. Your mother was the first of many women to have a huge weakness for you. She wrapped you up and nursed you with tenderness and love, and through her you learned how to be lovable and how to make someone love you. That knowledge has made you desirable to all other women.

You instinctively know how to behave with women, the right things to say to them. So they in turn love the way you behave and the way you talk. They appreciate the fact that you do justice to their cooking, that you are generous with your compliments. They are grateful that you don't constantly interrupt them or keep saying, 'See, I told you so', every time they do something stupid. You are very attentive, you anticipate their every little desire, you sense their insecurities. When she's with you, a woman always feels that she's the only one who really matters; you give the impression that you have always been there and that you always will be. It's all very reassuring.

Deep down, you understand women perfectly. You know that most of them would prefer a mixed salad to a bowl of brown rice. You also know that she can tolerate you using her toothbrush but she probably can't stand it if you keep changing the channels on the TV. Women love to feel that you are capable of taking care of them, and protecting them from the violence of the outside world. They also like to think that, on the other hand, you respect their independence. So you don't make a drama if she wants to go out alone one night with a friend or girlfriend. You don't feel threatened by her passion for her career or playing the piano or painting – on the contrary, you encourage her.

In fact, women love you almost unconditionally and their trust in you is almost unlimited. They pamper you and don't resent your failings. They find all sorts of excuses for you and easily forgive you your shortcomings. And if you do happen to disappoint them (which does occasionally happen – after all, nobody is perfect), they understand and probably even end up feeling totally responsible for it themselves.

Highest total Bs
Yes, women do love you really, but there is often an element of misunderstanding in your relations with them. You often feel that they don't love you as much as you think they should, or that you love them more than they love you. Your opinions of them go from one extreme to the other: either they are too intrusive, or they don't take enough care of you. You are suspicious that they are trying to take your freedom away, or encroach on your activities and your personal projects; or you think they want to keep you away from your friends. On the other hand, you feel sidelined by their desire to have children (or by the children themselves); and you hate it when they get too involved in their careers.

For their part, women would accuse you of liking the sound of your own voice just a little too much. They would say that you tend to force yourself on them when they don't feel like it. And they would maintain that you are too inclined to side with your mum when you should be supporting them. In short, your relationships are certainly passionate but not really harmonious.

It has to be said, though, that women often love you more than they realise. They miss you when you are not around. They hate it when they haven't got you there to bring them their breakfast in bed in the morning. They get used to hearing 'I love you' every day and when you break up, they're wrecked. They realise they are addicted to your spaghetti bolognese and think with nostalgia about the way you used to leave hairs in the bath.

You are not always on the same wavelength as your women, however. You sometimes have problems coming up to their expectations. You may share the same tastes and be sensitive to her desires, but you may not always be sufficiently attentive when she wants you to be, and you may have problems getting to grips with her perception of the right time for things. Women usually prefer to do things in their own time, and you need to be flexible in order to be able to take advantage of her spontaneous desires.

Learn to make concessions, and let your women love you.

Highest total Cs

No, women don't really love you. They say they do, they even believe it themselves, but it's not true. First of all because you are not terribly pleasant. You don't love women enough for them to feel loved. You find them possessive and, deep down, you don't understand them. You think it's enough to tell them that they are gorgeous and to give them an orgasm every now and then. In fact, they would prefer it if you didn't forget to say 'Thank you' or even 'Good morning' occasionally and if you would hold the door for them a bit more often. In terms of work around the house, they would much prefer that you didn't disappear every time the sink is blocked or the bed needs changing.

When a woman thinks she's in love with you, it's even worse. It's not you she really loves, but a certain image she has of you (and of herself). She loves you for all the wrong reasons: your income, your emotional weakness, your physical strength. You awaken her most unattractive instincts: greed, materialism and the desire to dominate you mentally and physically.

You have to make a bigger effort to be a little more lovable. For a start, you'll have to be more pleasant. It's not too difficult. Try to be a bit less selfish and a little more attentive, and try to pay her a few more compliments. And whatever you do, don't criticise her figure, don't keep interrupting her every three seconds, or swearing after every other word. Next – and this is a lot more difficult to do – avoid at all costs getting involved with women who are attracted by your assets, intoxicated by the smell of fresh money or excited by your emotional fragility. Put your Porsche and your complexes away. With a bit of luck and plenty of good manners, you will come across a woman who really loves you for what you are, even if you have got a few faults. (But bear in mind women aren't usually crazy about little fatties with greasy hair and glasses.)

Highest total Ds

Women really don't love you at all, not one bit: and usually they let you know. If you feel depressed, there's no way you could rely on one to comfort you or boost your ego.

If you've scored highly in this section, it's pretty much open war between you and women. They find you rude (you try to be too familiar too quickly), bad mannered (you push in front of them in queues) and horribly flashy (they're not overly keen on loads of gold chains or black hairs sprouting out of your shirt, which is open to the waist). They hate your attitude to the female sex (you're always coming out with little gems such as 'Women are hopeless drivers', 'Women just spend all their time on the phone' or 'What can you expect – she's a woman'). They loathe your ideas on marriage ('What's the longest sentence in the English language? – "I do".'). They despise your chronic infidelity and, in particular, your total lack of consideration.

You tend to treat women like cattle. So it doesn't really matter what you do, they regard you with deep suspicion. If you pay them attention, it's because you have an idea (usually a dirty one) in your head. If you give them a present, it's because you have done something wrong. You are never in their good books. Of course, sometimes they fall for your physique (especially if you are tall, slim and dark with blue eyes), but you still undress them a bit too much with your eyes and that tends to be a real passion-killer in the long run.

Of course, unless you are a total cynic, you must want women to love you more. Maybe not all of them (let's be realistic here) but at least some of them. But achieving that is going to be a long, hard slog for you. You are going to have to learn to listen to your woman, even when she bores on for hours; you'll have to compliment her on her cooking, even if it's just a microwaved frozen meal; you will have to say how good she looks, even if you think she's a mess; and you will have to give in to all her whims. In particular, stop asking her to share the bill when you're out for dinner (and refuse if she offers). Stop telling her she's pushy and overambitious when she's making a success of her job. And for heaven's sake, stop accusing her of behaving like a tart because she says 'Yes' or being frigid because she says 'No'.

DO YOU REALLY LOVE WOMEN?

A good EQ makes you more pleasant and more loved. It encourages other people, especially women, to feel well disposed towards you. How about you? How do you really feel about women? Do you really love them? Or, on the other hand, are they just accessories in your life? See for yourself.

Once again, read the following statements and choose your most likely response to each one.

SCORE:
Add up the number of As, Bs, Cs and Ds you score, then read the profile that corresponds to your highest total on pages 144–8. If you have less than two points' difference between totals, read both profiles.

You just love it when women:
- A Share your hobbies.
- B Scratch your back while you're making love.
- C Light up your weekends.
- D Fall asleep in your arms.

You think top models are rather:
- A Pretentious.
- B Unapproachable.
- C Annoying.
- D Artificial.

In your life, your top priority is:
- A Your work.
- B Your leisure time.
- C Your friends.
- D Your family.

You really hate women who:
- A Treat you like an idiot.
- B Only think about their job.
- C Collect guys.
- D Only think about going out.

If you were a pervert, you would :
- A Be a voyeur.
- B Take part in orgies.
- C Use chains and whips.
- D Be a fetishist.

A relationship means:
- A A power struggle.
- B Two lovers.
- C Two partners.
- D Two parents.

Things were better before, when women:
- A Wanted to be taken care of.
- B Weren't concerned with their careers.
- C Didn't turn and look every time an attractive man went past.
- D Were entirely wrapped up with their desire to have children.

As a child, you were:
- A Tormented by your sister(s).
- B Friends with your father.
- C Sent to boarding school.
- D Overprotected by your mother.

You once:
- A Had sex with a prostitute.
- B Called a sex line.
- C Went to see a porno film.
- D Pulled a girl on a chatline.

You would like a woman who:
- A Knows how to forgive.
- B Is understanding.
- C Has a sense of humour.
- D Is discreet.

Women are all:
- A Too materialistic.
- B Obsessed with their desire to have children.
- C Out to have their cake and eat it.
- D Too unpredictable.

Women should have more control:
- A Over themselves.
- B In the family.
- C In politics.
- D At work.

If a woman talks to you about her sexuality, you think it is:
- A Embarrassing.
- B Exciting.
- C Unremarkable.
- D Interesting.

If one of your fantasies could come true, you would choose:
- A Partner-swapping.
- B Having sex with another man.
- C Tying a woman up before making love to her.
- D Watching your girlfriend make love with another woman.

Your greatest fear is that one day:
    A You will have to work for a woman.
    B Your partner will leave you for another woman.
    C Your partner will earn more than you.
    D Women will run the country.

In your opinion, women prefer making love:
    A In the evening.
    B In the afternoon.
    C Any time.
    D In the morning.

To feel good, a woman has to make love:
    A Once a week.
    B Several times a day.
    C It depends on the woman.
    D Once a day.

Although you have never said so, you really think that:
    A Women are all tarts.
    B Women are inferior to men.
    C Women are totally unreliable.
    D Women haven't the faintest idea what they're doing.

Women take advantage of you, if you are too:
    A Kind.
    B Romantic.
    C Naive.
    D Honest.

You couldn't stand seeing the woman in your life:
    A Grow old.
    B Get fat.
    C Be unhappy.
    D Leave you.

You are a little disgusted by:
- A A woman who is having her period.
- B Pregnant women.
- C Women who are oversexed.
- D Prostitutes.

If you have a girlfriend, you shouldn't have to:
- A Hoover.
- B Empty the rubbish bin.
- C Iron your own shirts.
- D Sew on your own buttons.

The thing a woman most likes to do with her man is:
- A Go away for weekends with him.
- B Make love with him.
- C Talk with him.
- D Laugh with him.

You dream about being chatted up by:
- A An air hostess.
- B A model.
- C A woman you've never met.
- D Your (female) bank manager.

For a woman, you would be prepared to:
- A Stop smoking.
- B Be faithful.
- C Risk your life.
- D Move to another country.

The most exasperating thing about women is their:
- A Faddiness.
- B Constant questions.
- C Lies.
- D Lack of tolerance.

You love it when women are:
   A Vulnerable.
   B Provocative.
   C Intelligent.
   D Sweet.

When it comes to sex, you think:
   A It's important to be reassuring.
   B You have nothing to learn.
   C Women are much more demanding than they used to be.
   D You are always attracted by the same type of women.

Highest total As

You are a misogynist: it's rare to find someone who dislikes women more than you. Your hatred of women is not surprising, however. You were tyrannised by a domineering mother (or your father was), or persecuted by one or more harpy sisters. Obviously, that distorts your view of women and your attitudes to them.

Your first sexual experience was probably a failure. You didn't get an erection (you were too emotional) and you were utterly humiliated and disgusted. Now, after a few more unhappy experiences (you were never going to be much of a success considering your upbringing, your prejudices and your clumsiness), well, you just don't trust women. You don't have many women around you and you prefer relations with them to remain strictly professional. You need to protect yourself from them.

Liberated women, with their desires, impulses and excesses, scare you: you find them too unpredictable and completely unapproachable. You run away from emotional involvement, it unsettles you. In your life, women and any of their physical characteristics or functions have disappeared – they appear only in specific roles – wife, secretary, dentist, etc. All the women in your life have been picked with great care and you are very demanding of them but your relations with them are entirely sterile.

In love, you are often scared of getting carried away. Sexually, you need to control events, so you like to perform your own rituals, little ceremonial procedures that keep you detached from your partner. When you are aroused, you feel guilty. You always end up finding fault with women, sometimes without even knowing you are doing it – you hate the pleasure they give you, or the attachment you may feel for them. This applies as much to your secretary as to your wife. Furthermore, you tend to be possessive. You long for the old days when women were submissive and docile, when men didn't have to share their power. You are one of those hopeless men (and there are plenty of them still around) who are prepared to change their job or company rather than work for a woman; men who can't stand the fact that women are more successful professionally than them, that they can earn more. You are all for putting women back in the home where they belong. You are also one of those men who thinks that if a woman is attacked or raped, then she must have been asking for it (though you wouldn't say so out loud). There's no point telling you that the most liberated women are often the best – you just wouldn't believe it. It's sad that you will never know what you are missing.

Highest total Bs
You are a Don Juan: you think you love women, and you believe it all the more easily because they seem to run after you. Clearly, they occupy an important place in your life. You love to think about women and you dream about them a lot. You are full of admiration for them. You appreciate their patience (and they need a lot of it where you are concerned) and their delicacy and vulnerability. You think they are sweet and gentle creatures, you praise their capacity to forgive. For you, women are perfection – in your mind's eye. In reality, what you love is the idea of women, rather than women themselves. You love them in that they are indispensable to your ego; you need to have women in your life to stave off certain inferiority complexes.

In fact, you want them more than you love them. You need to seduce them to maintain your self-esteem, you need to persuade them to give in to you to prove to yourself you are truly virile. Subconsciously, you probably doubt it. Without sexual success, your own high opinion of yourself slumps. Clearly, no woman can satisfy you completely. You tend to lose interest in your conquests too quickly. What's more, you are very quick to reproach a woman for anything that you consider competes for her affection, makes her unavailable to you: her family, her job, her friends or even her desire to have a baby.

Your ego needs constant stroking. You are anxious about your ability to please or excite a woman so you have to keep proving that you can. Occasionally, you may really fall for a woman. When that happens, you get into a mother/child relationship, where you let yourself be mothered. You use women as emotional crutches, who constantly stimulate your ambitions and desires. But you don't really find it easy to bear this dependency and you respond by flying into frequent inexplicable rages. You are often unfaithful and show little consideration for her. In the end you make each other's life hell. But if you could only learn to be a little less self-centred, how different things might be.

Highest total Cs

To hear you talk, one would say that you hate women. You say they are capricious, fickle, intrusive, unpredictable. They don't keep their promises. They are either too aggressive (they think they are as good as the guys), or totally naive (they think they're in love just because a bloke makes a play for them). In short, they are untrustworthy and unreliable. You may sometimes even doubt that they are human at all – they don't seem to have a heart or a soul as far as you're concerned. It goes without saying that you think they are brainless, have no interest in anything intellectual and are fundamentally materialistic, acquisitive and essentially frivolous.

Leaving that aside, however, you quite often get a pang of desire when you pass a good-looking woman in the street. Femininity moves you. You already know all about men and their world; its familiarity bores you. So it is no surprise that you actually prefer to explore the world of women: it's a whole new universe, exciting in a different way. However, women do not find it easy to live with you. You like them to have plenty of character and personality, but you yourself are not very easygoing, rarely obliging, rather critical and demanding. Which obviously sometimes leads to sparks. You are not always very gentle either, you can be very harsh.

What you don't like about women is also what you don't like about men, yourself included. So when you don't get on with a woman, it makes you uncomfortable with yourself too. However, when things aren't going too well with your loved one, you don't usually make the mistake of thinking that the grass is greener somewhere else. At worst, you may seek temporary comfort in someone else's arms, but you don't believe that solves the problem. Deep down you have no illusions about the women you love. As someone once said: 'You don't need to be hopeful to undertake something, nor do you need to be successful to persist.'

Highest total Ds
You worship women, you love them to the extent that you often lose your sense of proportion or, more rarely, to the point of regretting not being one yourself. Wholly focused on love with a capital L, you have first and foremost a need to be loved by them. Your biggest fear is losing their love. To avoid this, you will try to make each day a new day full of surprises for them. You are attentive to their every need. You prefer to give in to them rather than upset them and you avoid confrontation of any sort. You are far too ready to oblige and you leap to your feet every time they bat an eyelid. You are the guy Napoleon was looking at when he said, 'Victory in love is in surrender.'

You are almost a slave to the woman in your life. She is the only one you want and dream about. You indulge her every whim, you agree with her, you feel kindly towards everything and everyone that concerns her. Even her mother, whom you think is a miracle. You don't have the words to thank her enough for having given birth to the queen of your heart. You would like to eat your loved one or be eaten by her to be more sure of keeping her.

You may be so enamoured of women that you are incapable of loving only one for very long. Your life may be a succession of long and deeply loving liaisons. You go from one passionate affair to another, keeping secret in your heart the memories of your past women. In years to come you will have rush of nostalgia, looking back on all those perfect times (you easily forget the bad ones). Clearly, women do what they want with you. You cannot refuse them anything. And, fortunately, whether it is due to their feminine intuition or pure good luck, you often choose women who return all the love you have for them.

PART 4

TEST YOUR RELATIONSHIP

ARE YOU MADE FOR EACH OTHER?

A good EQ leads to lasting relationships. Whether you have just met, or have been together for years, this section will help you and your partner probe deep into yourselves and find out if you really are on the same wavelength.

Both of you must do the test, but make sure you don't show each other your answers until you have finished. Then add up the number of As, Bs and Cs you each scored and read the profiles that correspond to both your highest scores.

For example, if you score most highly in As and he also scores highest in As, look at the section marked AA; if you score most highly in As and his highest score is Bs, see AB, and so on. Your letter always comes first.

SCORE:
Keep a note of both your scores and total up the number of As, Bs and Cs you score, then read the corresponding profiles on pages 153–7.

The best way to educate your children is to:
    A Make them face up to their responsibilities.
    B Bring them up the way your parents brought you up.
    C Always listen to them.

To feel good, you need to make love:
    A Once or twice a week.
    B Once every fortnight.
    C Three times a week or more.

Looking back on the first time you two met:
    A You both remember every little detail.
    B Your partner has only a vague recollection of it.
    C You never talk about it together.

It would kill your relationship if your partner was:
    A Selfish
    B Hypercritical.
    C Contemptuous towards you.

You argue:
    A Sometimes.
    B Rarely.
    C Often.

When you have an argument, the one to give in first is usually:
    A It depends, it's about even.
    B Your partner always gives in first.
    C Neither of you ever gives in.

You would say that you:
    A Tend to hold less of a grudge than your partner does.
    B Are good at forgiving.
    C Tend to hold quite a grudge.

When you make love:
    A Most of the time you reach a climax.
    B You're not really aware of much happening.
    C Your partner always climaxes before you.

When you make love, you particularly like to:
- A Take it slow and easy.
- B Go at it hammer and tongs.
- C Act out your sexual fantasies.

The worst thing your partner could do to you would be to:
- A Cheat on you.
- B Leave you.
- C Hit you.

A relationship cannot be a happy one, without a good measure of:
- A Goodwill and a mutual desire to please.
- B Effort.
- C Pleasure.

To make your partner stay, you would be most likely to say:
- A 'Let's give us a second chance!'
- B 'Think of the children!'
- C 'Think of what you're giving up!'

When your partner makes you angry, you are most likely to:
- A Disappear for three days without trace.
- B Throw your mother-in-law's gift china at them.
- C Start to cry.

You would be most likely to leave if your partner:
- A Went through your bag/pockets.
- B Insulted your mother.
- C Called you by someone else's name when you were making love.

When you are out for dinner:
- A You have different things but your partner lets you taste the dish they chose.
- B You often have the same thing.
- C Your partner often orders for you.

You take a bath or shower together:
    A Occasionally.
    B Never.
    C A lot.

You usually fall asleep:
    A Facing each other.
    B Curled round each other like spoons.
    C In each other's arms.

When there is a problem in your relationship:
    A You tackle it honestly together.
    B You discuss it with your parents.
    C You use your mutual friends as mediators.

When you were a child, you found talking to your parents about personal problems:
    A Easy.
    B Difficult.
    C Out of the question.

Having sex with someone means:
    A Enjoying an emotional and loving relationship.
    B Having children.
    C Having a good time.

Talking about sexuality with casual acquaintances is rather:
    A Interesting.
    B Embarrassing.
    C Exciting.

After making love you feel:
    A Good, relaxed.
    B Detached.
    C Sad, depressed.

Usually, the person who appears in your sexual fantasies is:
- A Your partner.
- B Someone with whom you had a sexual relationship in the past.
- C An imaginary person.

You would like to have a(nother) baby:
- A Maybe.
- B Yes, in a year's time.
- C No.

You believe it is most accurate to say that:
- A Love is built slowly, day by day.
- B There can be love in a relationship without sexual desire.
- C Infidelity can strengthen love.

If you scored AA

Yours is a marriage of convenience, the meeting of two self-sufficient but lonely people. You are determined to link up, to make the necessary concessions to build something together. Your relationship is a considered, logical and lasting one. You are both independent and have a lot of respect for each other's space and priorities. Not much in the way of enthusiasm or excesses, then.

You are both romantic, however, even if you sometimes don't allow yourselves any impulsive treats. You don't have arguments, or dramas, or scenes between you, or only a very few. If there's a problem, you are able to take a new look at yourselves, or you are each sufficiently intuitive to take the first step towards the other, which usually means everything gets settled. You are both prepared to compromise. You can be a little cold-blooded at times perhaps, but at least you are sure of being able to go far together.

If you scored AB

You have the same sense of shared responsibility, the same desire and strong will to build something lasting. You demonstrate infinite tenderness and real care towards each other, a concern for each other's well-being and pleasure. He has nice ways, pleasant manners, but also a tendency to get stuck in a routine – he has almost too much common sense and he is wedded to rather cautious habits. Hence your doubts and questions. When there's a problem, his self-confidence, his unbending attitude and inappropriate criticism of your view may quickly become hard to bear. Especially when he takes it into his head to tell you what to do or, even worse, he goes ahead and makes decisions without consulting you.

You two have some difficulties with each other: you may sometimes feel disillusioned and you will certainly have rows and dramas. But you never give up hope of teaching him the charm of looking at things from a woman's point of view, and eventually, you usually manage to win him over to your sense of the way things should be.

If you scored AC

You are not well matched. If you want to keep this man, you'll have to mother him. He's impulsive, a hostage to his emotions and his passions. Wild one day, submissive the next, he is difficult to reason with and hard to relate to. His desire for pleasure makes him ignore the realities of life. He needs to be taken in hand, to be supervised and guided, otherwise he will lose sight of what he is doing and end up running into someone else's arms, in his quest for new adventures. He can behave quite cruelly, without seeming to notice it. He may give you the impression that he thinks you are God's gift, but will his adulation last? Perhaps it will, if you have a plenty of patience and intuition. It definitely won't if you try to bring him down to earth. Rather selfish, he can take a lot but he gives very little in the end. Life with him feels like a game of roulette. You are too rational and too logical to stay with him for long. With time and experience, you will realise the extent of the problem and you may well decide it is not one that can be solved.

If you scored BB

You are a real mummy-daddy couple. You share the same desire to have children, preferably lots of them. Because of that you have a good chance of surviving the wear and tear of daily life together, and weathering the storms of time. By giving priority to your children, their well-being and education, you are able to cope with all your personal problems and to settle any conflict in your relationship without having a blazing row. Your disagreements are very much of an everyday nature. Of course, as a couple you agree on good family values, on things like teeth-brushing and good table manners. But we all tend to try to turn a situation to our advantage, and we may all be guilty of giving priority to our own family traditions, our own education, our own habits and preferences in our role as parents. So you will still have your power struggles, which will manifest themselves in a tendency to neglect each other in favour of children. But maybe you're not quite at that stage, maybe your children are yet to come ...

If you scored BA
He was a hardened bachelor, but he's fallen for your big eyes and your home cooking. His loneliness, his doubts about his place in life are all forgotten. He loves your warmth, your maternal attentions. The time has come for babies, DIY, Christmas at home with each other ... Yours is a relationship built on trust, hope and the will to make things work, even if at times he finds you a bit tyrannical (like your mother), rather possessive and not too realistic.

You sometimes accuse him of being too analytical and lacking spontaneity (he examines everything from every angle). You would prefer a little less objectivity and a bit more passion. But he's solid, dependable, hard-working and looks to the future. You see your life in very simple terms: what was good enough for your parents is good enough for you. He can sometimes be frustrating: he always has to be sure he has all the facts before he will do anything – and that even goes for having a baby.

If you scored BC
Yours is an almost incestuous relationship, with you playing the role of the domineering mother and him playing the role of a very

spoilt child. You are the one who takes care of all his problems, puts up with his fads and boosts his ego. And as soon as he feels comforted and reassured, he slips out of your possessive grip to escape from your constant lecturing and enjoy himself. He hates all kinds of rules and regulations, he wants to do just as he pleases. On the other hand, he depends on you and wants you to take charge and decide everything. He is either completely out of control, or completely docile, but either way it gets on your nerves and wears you out. You wish you didn't constantly have to lead him by the hand, you long for the day when he finally grows up so that you can trust him, rely on him, just have a break! In spite of all that, you do have a future together. In bed, at night, away from all the aggravation of your daily lives, you really do make each other very happy.

If you scored CA
Warning: this man is not for you. He can perform in bed, he has shown you how he can re-enact every scene from *9½ Weeks,* but he soon goes back to his books, his intellectual pursuits, his job (which is, of course, very important) and his own interests. He is as cold, logical and rational as you are passionate, impulsive and fun-loving. Of course you can adapt, if you are prepared to ignore everything in you that is natural and spontaneous, and give up your freedom. For his part, to be able to put up with you, he needs to ignore you, turn a blind eye. Under these conditions, your relationship doesn't have much of a future. Unless, of course, you are prepared to allow him to call the shots and content yourself with becoming his property, or party accessory. You are both worth more, you both deserve better than living life as a robot and a pet. On the other hand, miracles do happen. You each have an unusual enough personality and sufficient intelligence that you may learn to complement each other and so be able to make a lasting commitment to each other ...

If you scored CB
This is a father/daughter relationship. He is like a doting father and you are his spoilt little girl. You give him a hard time. He, in return,

indulges your every whim, soothes away all your problems, laughs at all your jokes. Or perhaps he is strict and tries to restrain you, constantly tells you off about your attitude and your infidelities (many of which he imagines). Whichever it is, your relationship may be long-lasting if he enjoys being paternalistic – he may be a bit of a Pygmalion and sufficiently easygoing to give you free rein when necessary. This is, of course, on condition that you play the game at least for the sake of appearances; let him think he is right, win him over with cuddles and kisses, have him wrapped round your little finger whilst still giving him the illusion that he's in charge. You must keep this up, otherwise in the long run he may tire of your egotism and feel frustrated and exploited. On the other hand, his quick temper, his kill-joy attitudes and his over-authoritarian treatment of you may make you feel that you don't want to put up with him any longer.

If you scored CC

Your relationship with him is a bed of roses, with the emphasis on the bed. It's all physical enjoyment, comfort, titillation, voluptuousness, sensual gratification, you are a pair of Epicureans. You act as if the present was going to last for ever. You don't care too much about building a solid foundation for your relationship. You're not interested so much in creating a family, as sharing your appetites for life and taking what you can get from it. You share a passion that shuts out the rest of the world and all its problems, but you are in danger of seeing your relationship self-destruct due to lack of real commitment or planning. Unless, of course, you have unlimited means for living a life of leisure.

With such strong emotional needs and desire for constant change, you may both find it hard to adapt to the constraints of real life. And in the end the frustration, resentment and disappointment you will inevitably experience will mean daily rows – and a lot of broken crockery. So unless you both thrive on this type of excitement, it's unlikely your relationship will be a long-term one.

Every Woman A Witch
by Cassandra Eason

In this fascinating and revealing book, Cassandra Eason demonstrates that any woman can boost the natural powers and female intuition which lie dormant within her. Magic itself is impossible to define, but *gut feeling, intuition, instinct* and *inspiration* are all in its train. Put together with positive mental attitude and they create a whole which can enable you to tap into new energies and make things happen.

Including: Outdoor Magic; Tree and Flower Magic; Crystal Magic; Sympathetic Workplace Magic; Candle Magic; Breaking a Bad Relationship; Love Spells; Sex Magic and Money Spells.

ISBN: 0-572-02223-9

A Woman Alone Can Be Contented
by Lynn Underwood

'If you are less than happy about life as a single person then believe me, it's all in your mind. I will show you how to make it what you want it to be. Single, certainly, but contented and self-fulfilled, too.

You don't need to waste the potential you have in living alone by wishing things were different. Let's accentuate the positive. I will show you how to plan a life with a healthy balance in all areas. And when you choose to enter a relationship, it will be much stronger for entering it without needing it.

I will show you that you can enjoy yourself and become happy and contented in your single life, as I have done.'

ISBN: 0-572-02267-0

Test your IQ

by Ken Russell and Philip Carter

Do you know your IQ? Not many people do. You may not be Mensa material, but it's interesting to work out just where you fit in.

This book offers 400 questions, arranged in a series of time-framed quizzes. The sum of your measurements for the tests will compound an average which shows how your IQ measures up.

You can treat the quizzes like an exam, or just enjoy gently taxing your brain power!

ISBN: 0-572-02484-3

Strengthen your Performance in Psychological Tests

by Cécile Césari

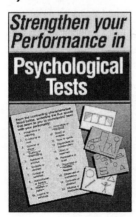

This is *the* book for job candidates. Here you will learn how the selection test works. You will learn about the elements which are fundamental to the selection process and how to handle them to better effect.

Including sample exercises with which to test yourself, become familiar with the most commonly used questions and build your confidence.

Césari reveals the essential thinking within the favoured selection tests: efficiency; personality; Rorschach project; intelligence; aptitude and sociability.

ISBN: 0-572-02208-5